Key Concepts in
Childhood Studies

The SAGE Key Concepts series provides students with accessible and authoritative knowledge of the essential topics in a variety of disciplines. Cross-referenced throughout, the format encourages critical evaluation through understanding. Written by experienced and respected academics, the books are indispensable study aids and guides to comprehension.

SECOND EDITION

Key Concepts in
Childhood Studies

ALLISON JAMES AND ADRIAN JAMES

Los Angeles | London | New Delhi
Singapore | Washington DC

Los Angeles | London | New Delhi
Singapore | Washington DC

SAGE Publications Ltd
1 Oliver's Yard
55 City Road
London EC1Y 1SP

SAGE Publications Inc.
2455 Teller Road
Thousand Oaks, California 91320

SAGE Publications India Pvt Ltd
B 1/I 1 Mohan Cooperative Industrial Area
Mathura Road
New Delhi 110 044

SAGE Publications Asia-Pacific Pte Ltd
3 Church Street
#10-04 Samsung Hub
Singapore 049483

Editor: Chris Rojek
Editorial assistant: Martine Jonsrud
Production editor: Katherine Haw
Copyeditor: Solveig Servian
Proofreader: Mary Dalton
Marketing manager: Michael Ainsley
Cover design: Wendy Scott
Typeset by: C&M Digitals (P) Ltd, India
Printed by: CPI Group (UK) Ltd,
Croydon, CR0 4YY

Library of Congress Control Number: 2012932301

British Library Cataloguing in Publication data

A catalogue record for this book is available from
the British Library

MIX
Paper from
responsible sources
FSC
www.fsc.org   FSC® C013604

ISBN 978-1-4462-0189-3
ISBN 978-1-4462-0190-9 (pbk)

contents

contents

key concepts in
childhood studies

contents

about the authors

Allison James is Professor of Sociology and Co-Director of the Centre for the Study of Childhood and Youth at the University of Sheffield. She is also Professor II at the Norwegian Centre of Child Research at the Norwegian University of Science and Technology (NTNU) in Trondheim. Allison James has worked in the sociology/anthropology of childhood since the late 1970s and has helped pioneer the theoretical and methodological approaches to research with children which are central to childhood studies. Her work focuses on children as social actors and her empirical research has included exploring children's language and culture in relation to theories of socialisation, children's attitudes towards sickness and bodily difference and children's experiences of everyday life at home and at school. Recent funded research has examined children's perceptions of hospital space and children as participants in family food practices. Currently, she is developing a child-centred approach to understanding socialisation. Key publications include: *Constructing and Reconstructing Childhood* (1990/1997). Basingstoke: Falmer (with A. Prout); *Theorising Childhood* (1998). Cambridge: Polity (with C. Jenks and A. Prout); *Research with Children* (2000). London: Falmer (with Pia Christensen); *Constructing Childhood: Theory, Policy and Social Practice* (2004). Basingstoke: Palgrave Macmillan (with A.L. James); *Children , Food and Identity* (2009). Basingstoke: Palgrave Macmillan (with A.T. Kjørholt and V. Tingstad).

Adrian James is Emeritus Professor of Applied Social Sciences at the University of Sheffield. He trained and practised as a probation officer and was subsequently extensively involved in their training. After becoming an academic in 1978, he researched and published widely in the field of socio-legal studies, including the completion of two major ESRC-funded projects on child welfare and divorce. Appointed as Professor of Applied Social Sciences at the University of Bradford in 1998, he became Professor of Social Work at the University of Sheffield in September 2004, during which time he was also Professor II at the Norwegian Centre for Child Research at the Norwegian University of Science and Technology (NTNU) in Trondheim. He was a Special Adviser to the House of Commons Select Committee on the Lord Chancellor's Department when it scrutinised the work of the Children and Family Court Advisory and Support Service (CAFCASS) in 2002–03. His recent books include: *Constructing Childhood: Theory, Policy and Social Practice* (2004). Basingstoke: Palgrave Macmillan (with Allison James); *The Child Protection Handbook* (3rd edn) (2007). London/Edinburgh: Elsevier/Ballière-Tindall (with K. Wilson): and *European Childhoods: Cultures, Politics and Childhoods in Europe* (2008). Basingstoke: Palgrave (with Allison James). The first edition of *Key Concepts in Childhood Studies* (also with Allison James) was published by Sage in 2008.

key concepts in childhood studies

preface

We are delighted to have had the opportunity to revisit our *Key Concepts in Childhood Studies* in the second edition of this book. This has given us the chance to add some new concepts that, somewhat mysteriously, we did not think to include first time round. Or perhaps it is the case that, with increasing interest being shown in childhood studies, as well as the changes occurring in childhood and for children themselves globally, these concepts have come into more prominent view since the first edition was published and now need to be given greater attention? Whatever the reason, we have now included 12 additional entries to make good this omission, though no doubt we could have added even more and some may yet disagree with the choices we have made about what, exactly, constitutes a key concept in childhood studies! However, we have also taken the opportunity to revise the original entries, updating them by including additional or new references where we have felt these were needed and, in some cases, expanding our original definitions through further material and cross-referencing.

We hope that, like the first edition, this volume will continue to prove a valuable resource for those who are new to childhood studies.

introduction

The title of this book is to a large extent self-explanatory – it seeks to define, introduce and explain to the reader in straightforward terms the key concepts that underpin the social study of childhood. In this sense, this book is intended to be a useful reference source for anyone wanting to study children and childhood in a social context. However, in the process of defining these key concepts, we have also sought to make clear the evolving political and social arenas in which childhood studies is located and the epistemological roots that support it. This is important, since the 'concepts' we explore are neither fixed nor free-standing; rather, they are embedded in particular social, cultural and historical contexts. This book represents, therefore, our own evolving understanding of children and childhood; the concepts we discuss are what, at this moment, seem to us to be the most important and influential ideas.

Many of the concepts we have identified and written about are not unique to childhood studies; they 'belong' to particular disciplines, such as sociology or psychology, or to the wider discourses of the social sciences, or even to the language of daily social life. As a consequence, we sometimes found that it was no easy task to define them before explaining them, precisely because, in many cases, their meaning is so widely understood. In framing the definitions we eventually decided upon, we occasionally struggled to find a new or different way of defining the relatively commonplace. On some occasions, we resorted therefore to standard sources of reference, such as dictionaries, for inspiration about where to start; on others, we found that the concepts had been so thoroughly deconstructed, refined and rehearsed in various public arenas that it proved almost impossible not to draw upon definitions about which there is now a wide consensus. In each and every case, however, we have sought to build upon the common meanings or definitions of these terms, in order to identify what is different or problematic about them and how they are used and understood in the context of childhood studies.

This, too, tells us a lot about childhood studies. Part of the challenge confronting the pioneers in this field has been to problematise that which is self-evident – namely, children and childhood. Children and childhood are so integral to the human experience and the human life-course that we can all claim to be 'experts by experience', many of us as parents and all of us as children. However, rather than being an advantage, this prior, everyday knowledge complicates the process of *studying* children and childhood because we may find it difficult to set this knowledge aside. One of our aims in the book has been, therefore, to enable the reader to think carefully and reflexively about concepts which they may think they already know by casting new light on taken-for-granted ideas about children and childhood.

Another of our starting points has been the acknowledgement that childhood is a complex phenomenon, which therefore requires complex understandings that cannot be arrived at by looking through a single disciplinary lens. This, too, has been a challenge for us. Given our own disciplinary backgrounds, it is inevitable that we have tended to favour the perspectives of sociology and social anthropology in exploring the various concepts we have included in this volume. We are clear, however, that even though it might be argued with some justification that child-hood studies owes most in terms of its theoretical development to sociology, child-hood studies must be conceived of as an area of interdisciplinary scholarship. Our choice of key concepts recognises that history, geography, psychology, economics, medicine, social policy, law, pedagogy, art and literature have all also made impor-tant contributions to the study and understanding of children and childhood. Taken together, these provide a multi- and interdisciplinary framework within which the different parameters of childhood and the lives of children can be studied.

This does not mean that the concepts explored here are exhaustive, for there are other players in the childhood field that receive less attention in this volume. For example, there has been a long-standing research interest in the field of *early* child-hood studies. Primarily, this work is concerned to study young children during the early stage of the life-course to enable adults in general, and teachers in particular, to be more effective and efficient in terms of child-rearing and social pedagogy. In this sense, this work can often have a very particular and instrumental framing. Childhood studies, as represented by the concepts included in this book, is conceived of in much broader terms; it is concerned with the social study of all childhoods and all children of all ages, in their own right and not just as a means to an end.

It has also been important for us in identifying what are, indeed, the *key* con-cepts in childhood studies, to acknowledge the contribution made by the chil-dren's rights 'movement', which has a very different, although arguably complementary, agenda. The growth of interest in children's rights received a major boost from the United Nations Convention on the Rights of the Child (UNCRC) 1989, which has provided the focus for much debate and research into the lives of children. This has become an important focus of the research carried out by many non-governmental organisations around the world and has made use of the research and theorising done in the field of childhood studies more gener-ally. Childhood studies has, in turn, also come to draw on the conceptualisations of children's rights, capabilities and participation developed by researchers from these organisations, which has led to some blurring of the lines between 'research' and 'action'.

However, although childhood studies has many overlaps with both the agenda of early childhood studies and the children's rights movement, as an area of schol-arship its aims are rather different. The primary concern of childhood studies is to extend our knowledge and understanding of childhood and its complexities, rather than to engage directly in social or political interventions in children's lives. This is not, of course, to suggest that the study of childhood is or should be entirely self-referential and that its sole purpose is its own theoretical development; it is both proper and desirable that the insights and understandings gained from such research should be applied in the social world. It is possible, however, to argue that childhood studies must be able, and must safeguard its capacity, to look beyond application for its raison d'être. Thus the concepts we have chosen to explore reflect this aim and purpose and, in this sense, they do not constitute a comprehensive reference source for all the research work and interest that there is in children and childhood today.

This, then, is the perspective on childhood studies that is presented through the key concepts explored in this volume. Defining any developing field of study in this way is an inherently risky venture; precisely because it is developing, there will be those who disagree with our selection of what we believe to be the key concepts, or our understanding of these, or both. In our view, this is a risk worth taking, not least because if our attempts to define the social study of childhood do lead to challenges and disagreements, this will lead to debate and to further clarification. And it is through such a process that new fields of academic endeavour evolve and mature and eventually come to realise their full potential. This, ironically, provides us with a metaphor for childhood itself, as a developmental stage in a process of growth towards maturity. Only in retrospect, and at a later stage in the life-course of childhood studies, will we eventually be able to judge the adequacy of the key concepts that we have chosen to describe in terms of their contribution to the growth of this important area of study.

HOW TO USE THIS BOOK

The concepts are arranged alphabetically and each begins with a very short definition. However, often the concepts are not straightforward in the sense that there may be differing views about their range and application, or the concepts may be controversial in other ways. The explanations that follow therefore set out these issues and seek to highlight, for example, the different sides to a debate or to chart the changes in the ways in which a concept has developed over time.

In addition, many concepts are interrelated. It is sometimes necessary, therefore, to refer to other concepts in discussing their meaning and relevance for childhood studies. Where this happens, we have cross-referenced to these other concepts by emboldening them in the text, so that you can look up these other entries to get a fuller picture.

At the end of each section you will find a list of the references used in the text plus some further reading. This list includes some of the key classic texts that have informed the development of the concept as well as more up-to-date references. It is, however, in no way exhaustive, since it is only intended to provide a brief indication of the range of available material. You should use this list as a springboard to explore more widely the ways in which any particular concept has been informed by research.

As you read about the concepts, you will notice that we have tried, wherever possible, to offer an international perspective, drawing examples of the relevance of the concept from places outside of Europe and the USA. In particular, we have been keen to explore the relevance of our key concepts for childhoods outside of the West for, in terms of the global population of children, the western experience of affluent childhood – despite its dominance over our thinking – is a minority experience. For this reason, when we draw comparative examples of childhood in Africa or Asia or other poorer regions of the world, we refer to these by using the description 'the majority South', which is the preferred terminology now used by NGOs who work in these regions.

Finally, although we set out to explore concepts that cover not only the key themes within childhood studies, but also ones that are pertinent to understanding all children's experiences of childhood everywhere, there will be instances where we have failed. We urge you to use this book not as an authoritative text that closes off discussion but rather as a reference point, a springboard of ideas that enables you to think through the relevance of these key concepts for the particularities of the childhoods that you are seeking to understand.

Allison James and Adrian James
Department of Sociological Studies, University of Sheffield

Age and Maturity

> *The number of years a person has lived.*

Although in contemporary western societies age is commonly regarded as a fundamental aspect of a person's identity and is calculated numerically in terms of the
passage of years since birth, this reckoning of time passing is not universal. Neither
has it always been regarded as significant. In this sense, age can be regarded as one
of the ways in which the passage of time across an individual's life-course is
socially constructed. The historian Gillis (1996) argues, for example, that in western Europe it was only in the late 19th century that age became an important
marker of social identity within the life-course. Prior to that, a person's chronological age might bear little relationship to the kinds of expectations and experiences that people had. So, unlike today, the pattern of life-course transitions was
not fixed according to numerical age. Thus, for example, starting **work**, and then
later marriage, did not always follow on from finishing attendance at school.
Rather, boys and young men (though this was not so often the case with girls and
women) might go in and out of school over a long period of time, taking up work
in-between times, as their personal circumstances dictated. Thus, as Aries (1962)
notes, the term '**child**' was traditionally not an age-related term; instead, it was
more often used to describe a person's social dependency upon another.

In the modern world, however, as Hockey and James (2003) observe, there has
been an increased institutionalisation of chronological age within the life-course
and age is now key to the definition of what a child is:

> [F]rom legal imperatives through to consumer practices, age consciousness has inten-
> sified, such that what it means to be a child, for example, has become highly contex-
> tualized in relation to the age of criminal responsibility, consensual sex, leaving
> school, consent to surgery, access to contraception, participation in work and the
> right to vote. (2003: 64)

Although age is regarded as a key definitional marker of the status of 'child', when
used to try to describe the lived experiences of children, age is revealed to be a less
useful concept for a number of reasons. The first reason lies in the ways in which
biological age has been used to chart out children's physical, psychological and
indeed social development. Clearly, children share a common trajectory of physical
change and development over time that is largely age-based, so that children
achieve different stages of motor skills at different ages. Toddlers usually crawl
before they walk, and may do this from around nine months old. However, the
mapping of an age- and stage-based categorisation schema on to children's social,
intellectual and psychological development, irrespective of social context, is now
regarded as problematic. Not all children achieve the same stages at the same age,

age and maturity

1

albeit that new research focused on **developmentalism** is shedding further light on the broad developmental changes that occur in the brain during childhood and adolescence. Nonetheless, age-grading remains a fundamental aspect of the ways in which, in modern society, children's lives are structured, because what the calculation of numerical age permits is the establishment of uniformly applicable boundaries to separate children from adults in particular cultural contexts.

The **school** system in many countries provides a prime example of age becoming institutionalised in this way. Schools divide children into different age-based classes, usually structured in relation to the annual intakes of children into the school system, ranging from early childhood through to the school-leaving age. Different age classes study different curricula, with different standards set for children's achievement. The result of this process is, however, to establish a process of age-based standardisation (James, 2004) such that some children may come to be judged as failing, as being 'behind' or 'backward' for their age, while others may be regarded as 'gifted' or 'precocious' because they achieve more than would have been expected *for their age*.

The second problem associated with the concept of age arises when it is used to define 'the child' and, through doing so, to place restrictions or protections on, or to give permissions for, children's activities. Not only does this place children of the same age together in the same group, irrespective of the differences among them, it also means that when age is used in this way, in a legal context, different ages may be used as boundary definitions for 'the child' in different social contexts. In relation to children's **rights**, for example, the **United Nations Convention on the Rights of the Child (UNCRC) 1989** defines a child as a person under the age of 18. Given the rather different social and economic circumstances that children across the world experience, such a universalising, age-based definition is problematic since it implies a commonality of experience that is not there. For example, the ages for consensual sex, for getting married and for leaving school vary enormously among different countries, and some **working children** of the majority South may enter the adult workplace at a very young age. But even within a single society, there may be little consistency about age-based definitions of 'the child'. In England, for example, within the youth justice system, a child is now deemed to be competent and responsible for his or her actions from the age of 10. In terms of the **welfare** system, however, children up to the age of 18 may not have their wishes and feelings taken notice of if it is thought that to accede to these may not be in their **best interests**.

This use of age to define 'the child' also raises issues in relation to ideas of maturity. While maturity can be defined in relation to developmentalism – for example, the achievement of sexual maturity –it is also commonly used to make a qualitative assessment or judgement about a child's actions, thoughts or behaviour. Indeed, 'maturity' describes the extent to which a child appears to behave or think more as an adult does. Thus, for example, when a child is described as being 'mature' for her/his age, the suggestion is that they are behaving more competently than would normally be expected of a child of that age. Maturity, then, is in effect a social construction and, as a consequence, understandings of what counts as 'maturity' are culturally relative. Notwithstanding the considerable problems that this raises for global childhoods, Article 12 of the UNCRC assumes that 'maturity' is something that, like 'age', can somehow be objectively assessed: 'States Parties shall assure to the child who is capable of forming his or her own views the right to express those views freely in all matters affecting the child, the views of the child being given due weight in accordance with the age and maturity of the child.' This is just one of the many examples of the problems that arise when trying to implement the UNCRC at the local level since what counts as evidence of ' maturity' in one setting may not in another.

Finally, age can also be problematic when seen from a child's **standpoint** since it may, for the reasons noted above, restrict children's activities. Solberg's (1997) study of Norwegian children shows, for example, how 10-year-old children manage to negotiate their parents' perceptions of their 'age'. By carrying out household tasks with **competence**, some children, she argues, act 'older' than their age, leading their parents to trust them to be alone in the house. In this way, through their everyday actions and interactions, these Norwegian children transformed age into a relative concept and circumvented the restrictions that fixed, numerical age can place upon them.

Age as a classificatory marker of identity has become, therefore, particularly important for children, since it is used not only to separate them out as a special group in society, but it may also restrict the kinds of activities and social **spaces** to which they have access. Indeed, many contemporary concerns about children's access to the **internet** and the **sexualisation** of children are underscored by views about age appropriateness and ideas about children's relative maturity and immaturity.

FURTHER READING

Aries, P. (1962) *Centuries of Childhood.* London: Jonathan Cape.
Gillis, J.R. (1996) *A World of Their Own Making.* Oxford: Oxford University Press.
Hockey, J. and James, A. (2003) *Social Identities Across the Life-Course.* Basingstoke: Palgrave.
James, A. (2004) 'The standardized child: Issues of openness, objectivity and agency in promoting child health', *Anthropological Journal on European Cultures*, 13: 93–110.
Solberg, A. (1997) 'Changing constructions of age for Norwegian children', in A. James and A. Prout (eds), *Constructing and Reconstructing Childhood* (2nd edn). London: Falmer.

agency

3

The capacity of individuals to act independently.

The idea that children can be seen as independent **social actors** is core to the development of the new paradigm for the study of children and young people that emerged in the social sciences during the 1970s. It underscores children's and young people's capacities to make choices about the things they do and to express their own ideas. Through this, it emphasises children's ability not only to have some control over the direction their own lives take but also, importantly, to play some part in the changes that take place in society more widely. As Mayall describes it, a focus on children's agency enables exploration of the ways in which children's interaction with others 'makes a difference – to a relationship or to a decision, to the workings of a set of social assumptions or constraints' (2002: 21).

The concept of agency is important for **childhood studies** for two reasons. First, it illustrates the significant links that this relatively new interdisciplinary area has with wider theoretical debates within the social sciences. Second, it draws attention to some of the new ways of thinking about children and young people that have enabled recent research and policy perspectives to be developed. These have not only widened our understanding of childhood, but also had benefits for children themselves. We shall turn our attention first to sociological theory.

Discussions of agency within sociology form part of what is known as the structure–agency debate that has a long history within the social sciences. Stretching back to the different theoretical perspectives initiated by Karl Marx, Max Weber and Émile Durkheim, this debate is, in essence, a struggle to evaluate the competing claims made about the extent to which individuals can act independently of the social **structures**, institutions and value systems that make up the societies in which they live. For both Durkheim and Marx, for example, society was seen as overarching, as determining what people do through the various constraints that collective moral ideas and social institutions place upon their actions. For Durkheim, the 'conscience collective' framed a people's way of thinking about the world, while for Marx, famously, it is not the people's consciousness that determines their social being but their position as social beings, as members of society, that determines their consciousness and ways of thinking.

Max Weber, by contrast, was more concerned to explore society from the perspective of those who live in it. In his view, it is the meanings that people attribute to their social actions and events that help structure the nature of society. In this sense, a Weberian perspective offers perhaps the greatest insight into ideas of agency, given its focus on social action, although from a Durkheimian or Marxist perspective, it is arguable whether people are as free to act and make meanings as the Weberian model implies.

This long-standing and difficult struggle to evaluate the relative weight of the effects of 'structure' on people's capacity to act freely has led theorists to attempt to reconcile these positions, and to argue that both structure and agency are important. Anthony Giddens's (1979) work on structuration theory is perhaps the best-known example. Giddens suggests that structure and agency cannot be seen as stand-alone concepts since they are irrevocably intertwined; social structures provide the means through which people act, but the form these structures take is a result of their actions. In this sense, social life is not only reproductive, in terms of both the continuity of structures and institutions, but also potentially transformative. People can and do have the power, through their actions, to change the very social structures and institutions through which they have to live and **work**. Critical realists such as Bhaskar argue, however, that such a view downplays the historical dimension. They maintain that the capacity of structures and institutions to endure and to act as very material constraints upon people's actions, as well as to offer a variety of opportunities for change, is not really developed sufficiently within structuration theory. Martin and Dennis (2010), on the other hand, reject such dualist thinking altogether, suggesting instead that what is needed is a focus on the ways in which people's lives are embedded in social relations and processes of different kinds.

The significance of these different theoretical positions for understanding the capacity of children for agency and also their potential effectiveness as agents should not be under-estimated (Valentine, 2011). Indeed, James et al. (1998) outline a schematic model that identifies the different ways in which both structure and agency have influenced how children are seen. However, given the longstanding sway which traditional **socialisation** theory has held over the study of children and childhood, in which children were so often positioned as passive receivers of society's messages, it is important to consider the different ways in which children's agency might be conceptualised.

For some researchers, children's agency is seen as a function of their role as **social actors**. Here the concept of agency draws attention to children's subjectivities as independent social actors within the social, moral, political and economic constraints of society. In his research on the role of **ethnicity** and **gender** in young children's everyday lives, Connolly, for example, is keen to show 'how competently and with what complexity the children are able to appropriate, rework and reproduce racist discourses in relation to a variety of situations and contexts' (1998: 5). In particular, he explores how cultural ideas of race are articulated differently by boys and girls within the school context leading, for example, to black boys foregrounding an assertive masculinity, while black girls use ideas of femininity to downplay wider cultural stereotypes about the 'volatile and aggressive nature of Black girls' (1998: 15). Through exploring children's agency, Connolly shows how race as a social and cultural marker of identity is subtly transformed by children in and across the varying contexts of their everyday lives.

Other researchers, by contrast, are concerned to explore agency in the context of structure's constraining influence, which shapes children's collective position as a **minority group** in society. Mayall (2002), for example, discusses children's agency and their ability to act as agents in relation to their **generational** position vis-à-vis adults. In her view, the fact that children's agency is not generally acknowledged by the adult world is something that not only contributes to children's minority social status but also shapes children's subjectivities and therefore helps reproduce their relative powerlessness. In her research she discovered, for example, that although children reveal themselves to be capable moral agents, 'able and willing to take account of other people's views … and [to] put aside their own immediate interests with the aim of helping others', they did not 'give themselves credit for their own moral agency' (2002: 110). This, Mayall argues, both reflects and refracts their subordinated structural position within the generational order.

This latter perspective raises a number of questions about the extent to which children are able to exercise their agency and the effect that this might have upon society. To what extent do – and can – children contribute to social change? Are they outside the **cultural politics** of any society or can the things that children do, either as individuals or as a group, have an impact upon society, instigating processes of social transformation, as well as social and cultural reproduction?

FURTHER READING

Connolly, P. (1998) *Racism, Gender Identities and Young Children*. London: Routledge.
Giddens, A. (1979) *Central Problems in Social Theory*. London: Macmillan.
James, A., Jenks, C. and Prout, A. (1998) *Theorizing Childhood*. Cambridge: Polity.
Martin, P.J. and Dennis, A. (2010) *Human Agents and Social Structures*. Manchester: Manchester University Press.
Mayall, B. (2002) *Towards a Sociology of Childhood: Thinking from Children's Lives*. Buckingham: Open University Press.
Valentine, K. (2011) 'Accounting for agency', *Children & Society*, 25(5): 347–59.

Best Interests

> The yardstick by which decisions relating to children and their rights under the **UNCRC** are made.

The United Nations Convention on the Rights of the Child (**UNCRC**), drawn up in 1989, contains a wide range of provisions relating to different **rights** for children, rights which all the States that have signed up to the Convention agree to support. None of these rights, in principle, is more important than any other. The provisions of Article 3 of the Convention, however, which requires a commitment to determining issues in the best interests of the child, have assumed the status of a general principle, in that they underpin all of the other provisions of the Convention. Article 3 states that:

> In all actions concerning children, whether undertaken by public or private social welfare institutions, courts of law, administrative authorities or legislative bodies, the best interests of the child shall be a primary consideration.

Several points are worth noting about this. The first is its reach: the best interests principle encompasses not just official organisations and departments of State, it also embraces legal, legislative, judicial and regulatory bodies, as well as private and charitable bodies concerned with children's **welfare**. The second is its comprehensiveness: it is intended to guide *all* actions concerning children, not just specified and thus selected actions. This means that signatories should not give a higher priority to the best interests of the child in some areas than in others; in this way it provides the basis on which *all* of the other provisions of the Convention are to be interpreted. The third point worth noting is the weight to be given to the principle: under the provisions of Article 3, the best interests of the child are a *primary* consideration. In other words, they are not the *only* consideration that can be brought to bear in determining actions in relation to children: they may be one of several, and they are not the *paramount* or even the first consideration, only a primary consideration, that is, one of the first.

In respect of children's rights, the provisions of the UNCRC offer a significant improvement over the provision of other Conventions, such as the European Convention on Human Rights 1950. This contained no similar provisions relating to children's best interests. Nonetheless, in spite of its comprehensiveness, the careful drafting of Article 3 inevitably weakens its potential impact, since it allows concern for 'the best interests of the child' to be set alongside other possibly competing considerations. For example, when considering responses to **delinquency** and offending by children and young people, issues of public safety and social control might be seen as determining decisions in relation to children over and above their best interests.

A further limitation is that the UNCRC also offers no guidance on the meaning and interpretation of the principle of the best interests of the child, which has become a *leitmotif* in discourses about children's welfare. This is significant because it allows children's best interests to be understood in the context of their **protection**, and in this sense they are open to different interpretations. One consequence of this is that children's **participation** rights under Article 12 (which gives children the right to participate in decisions that affect their future) can be readily subordinated to adult judgements about what is in their best interests where children are deemed to be in need of protection. That the best interests principle is also commonly referred to as the 'welfare principle' reveals the significance of this lack of guidance. It allows children's best interests to be determined in terms of their welfare and, for example, enables adults to override any wishes and feelings children themselves may have expressed about wanting to participate in decision-making processes. There is also the risk that the term 'best interests' has become so widely incorporated into so many other discourses, including many that are closely related to adults' concerns and interests (see, for example, James, 2003), that it may become devalued and relegated to the status of rhetoric.

In spite of such limitations and risks, the significance of the best interests principle is its centrality to the other provisions of the UNCRC and thus the imperative to place children's interests at the very heart of a wide range of decisions that affect them.

FURTHER READING

Fortin, J. (2003) *Children's Rights and the Developing Law* (2nd edn). London: LexisNexis/ Butterworths. (Chs 1 and 2.)

Franklin, B. (2002) *The New Handbook of Children's Rights.* London: Routledge.

best interests

James, A.L. (2003) 'Squaring the circle – the social, legal and welfare organisation of contact', in A. Bainham, B. Lindley, M. Richards and L. Trinder (eds), *Children and their Families: Contact, Rights and Welfare*. Oxford: Hart.

James, A. and James, A.L. (2004) *Constructing Childhood: Theory, Policy and Social Practice*. London: Palgrave.

Van Bueren, G. (1995) *The International Law on the Rights of the Child*. The Hague: Martinus Nijhoff.

Child

> *A child is a human being in the early stages of its life-course, biologically, psychologically and socially; it is a member of a generation referred to collectively by adults as 'children', who together temporarily occupy the social space that is created for them by adults and referred to as 'childhood'.*

As Chris Jenks (1996) has argued, we cannot imagine the child except in relation to a conception of the adult and, conversely, it becomes impossible to generate a well-defined sense of the adult, and indeed adult society, without starting with the idea of the child. So what are the distinctive differences between a child and an adult? Children are, in most cases, less well-developed physically than adults: they tend to be shorter, to weigh less, and in the case of younger children, have yet to develop the secondary sexual characteristics associated with their **gender**. Children are also, in most cases, less well-developed mentally than adults in terms of their intellectual abilities, cognitive skills, the breadth and depth of their knowledge, and their ability to understand and to reason. In addition, children tend to be less well-developed both psychologically and socially: compared to adults, they tend to be less emotionally mature, less socially skilled, less articulate and less competent in terms of life-skills.

It is from these characteristics of children, as a *biological* and *social* category, that we derive our definition of what it is to be an adult – literally to be 'a grown-up'. Moreover, because these are primarily developmental criteria, the process of growing up and ageing makes **age** a key factor in how we differentiate a child from an adult. Thus 'adulthood', and accompanying notions of personhood and **citizenship**, come not through achievement or competence but through ageing.

The differentiating factors described above serve to underline one of the main problems in defining the child using such developmental and age-based criteria: they lack precision. It is necessary in relation to each variable to qualify it, with phrases such as 'in most cases' or 'tend to', since no descriptor is sufficient on its own, or even when considered along with other variables. Thus, it is possible to have adults who are shorter, less heavy and less socially or psychologically developed than some whom we know, by virtue of their age, to be children. It is equally possible to have children who are taller, heavier and/or better mentally developed than some adults.

Even age is not necessarily helpful in defining a child, although it is widely used for definitional purposes. Thus, for example, Europe recently adopted the definition of a child as 'any person below the age of 18' (European Council Framework Decision 2004/68/JHA, 22.12.2003). Most societies, however, would recognise some distinction between infants and toddlers on the one hand and **youth**/adolescents on the other, both in terms of the age criterion and the developmental indicators outlined above. Consequently, comparisons are frequently drawn between children and young people in order to make meaningful distinctions that can guide particular social actions, such as dealing with **delinquency** or the formulation of youth policy. And yet for other purposes, such as education or child **protection**, these different categorisations might be subsumed under the overarching categorical label of 'child'.

To complicate things even further, as the process of physical maturation in western industrialised societies occurs at ever younger ages, and the age at which full social and economic independence is achieved occurs ever later, we have seen the emergence (or creation) of yet a further category of child: the 'tweenies' or 'tweenagers' (Wyness, 2006). This group, who are no longer young children but are still not yet adolescents, constitute a category that is arguably the construction of retail companies, who have recognised **children as consumers** and the considerable spending power of 10 to 13-year-olds in relation, for example, to food and clothing.

Hence, in defining 'child', we do not and cannot limit ourselves to locating the child in terms of the early developmental stage of the life-course, since this is clearly insufficient. It is necessary to refine this by acknowledging the importance of social and cultural contexts and practices that, in addition to age and developmental criteria, define the child, children and **childhood** (Lee, 2001). It is through these also that the child is defined in any given society at any given point in history. At the same time, it is these same social, cultural and legal practices, embodied in the **cultural politics of childhood**, that serve to define our understanding of what it is to be an adult, with all that this implies in terms of citizenship status and **rights**. And, finally, it is the combination of all of these that has enabled discussion of the **social construction** of childhood and of the idea of the child as **culturally relative**.

FURTHER READING

Alanen, L. and Mayall, B. (eds) (2001) *Conceptualizing Child–Adult Relations*. London: Routledge/Falmer.

European Council Framework Decision 2004/68/JHA, 22.12.2003 on combating the sexual exploitation of children and child pornography. *Official Journal of the European Union*, L 13/44-48, 20.1.2004.

Hunt, S. (2005) *The Life Course: A Sociological Introduction*. Basingstoke: Palgrave Macmillan.

Jenks, C. (1996) *Childhood*. London: Routledge.

child

9

Lee, N. (2001) *Childhood and Society: Growing Up in an Age of Uncertainty*. Buckingham: Open University Press.

Wyness, M. (2006) *Childhood and Society: An Introduction to the Sociology of Childhood*. Basingstoke: Palgrave Macmillan.

Child-focused Research/ Research with Children

Research that is conducted with children as the subjects, rather than the objects, of research.

Prior to the growth of **childhood studies**, with its emphasis on children as **social actors**, childhood research was carried out most commonly by **developmental psychologists** interested in child growth and development, or by sociologists interested in processes of **socialisation** under the auspices of **family** sociology. In neither of these instances were children readily seen as research subjects who might have a point of view to articulate or as people who could be actively involved as participants in the research process. Woodhead and Faulkner (2007), for example, chart the gradual shift, within developmental psychology, from researchers viewing children simply as objects of scientific experimentation, through to research, such as that carried out by Jean Piaget, that began to see children as research subjects who might be interviewed and listened to. In the context of sociology, the new paradigm within childhood studies, outlined by Prout and James in 1997, not only positioned children as 'active in the construction and determination of their own lives, the lives of those around them and of the societies in which they live' but also recognised that children could have 'a more direct voice and participation in the production of sociological data' (1997: 8).

Such a shift in perspective has enabled children's views and ideas to become the central focus of research, inspiring the description of such work as being 'child-centred'. And indeed, this description is often used interchangeably with the term 'child-focused'. Whichever term is used to describe a piece of research, what is important are the methods and the ethical stance that have been adopted. Child-focused research is not simply about doing research about children; it must adopt methods and ethical procedures that respect children as research participants in their own right, and adhere to this value throughout the research process.

One way in which this can be achieved is through adopting participatory research techniques that enable children's **participation** in the research process by making that process more meaningful to them (Tisdall et al., 2009). In research that sought out children's experiences of the care system, O'Kane (2007) describes, for example, how the research team developed decision-making charts to help children express their feelings about the decisions that had been taken for them by the various adults involved in their lives, such as social workers and parents. Using coloured stickers placed on a gridded chart, the children were able to construct for themselves – and for the researchers – a visual map of those people who had the most 'say' in the decision-making process and those who had the least. Using this technique, children had time to reflect on their experiences and to tell the researcher about things that were important to them. In this case, it was discovered that, from the children's perspectives, the everyday decisions – about where they were allowed to go or what they did – were just as significant as the longer-term decisions being made about their futures. Alison Clark, together with her colleague Peter Moss, developed what they termed 'the Mosaic approach' to such participatory research. This involves the use of a wide range of methods that 'enable children and adults to be active participants in the research rather than depend on the researcher becoming an active participant in the research participants' lives' (Clark, 2010: 33).

However, child-focused research does not necessitate the use of such innovatory methods. What is needed is an appreciation of children's **standpoint** in the research process. Mayall (2002), for example, describes her research with children as a set of conversations that she joined in with, conversations that children had already been having with their friends – about their parents, about family life and so on. What the 'relatively formal character of the research conversation allowed', she argues, was the 'fuller development of ideas than might always be the case in their own informal conversations' (2002: 121). In later one-to-one interviews with individual children, the conversations became more personal because, Mayall suggests, of the age difference between the older researcher and the younger informant.

In this observation, Mayall highlights a key dimension that has to be carefully negotiated in child-focused research: the potential problems raised by the age and power differentials inherent between children and adults. While some, such as Mandell (1991), have suggested that it is possible to play a 'least-adult' role when carrying out research with children, when even physical size differences between adult and child can be downplayed, others disagree. They suggest instead that it is only a different adult role that can be achieved. Corsaro and Molinari (2007) describe, for example, how long-term ethnographic fieldwork enabled Bill Corsaro, as the researcher, to wait for the children to invite him into their **social worlds** as some kind of strange but kindly adult, rather than as a pseudo-child. The children could always exclude him from their world by referring to his adult status.

Another key dimension of child-focused research is the ethical dimension, whereby children are respected as people able to give – and to withdraw – consent at all stages of the research process. To enable this, Alderson and Morrow (2004) have produced a set of questions that need to be considered when carrying out child-focused research. Much research with children is carried out in the **school** context, for example. This is a place where children are used to living within a hierarchical and authoritative system where, quite often, they have little say or control. While formal permission for research has usually to be obtained from the school head or education authority and also from children's parents or guardians, child-focused research must also confirm children's own informed consent to participate in the research. Within schools this can be difficult since children may feel obliged to agree, given the pressure for conformity and obedience that permeates many schools, or teaching staff may insist that all children take part. As Alderson and Morrow note, these and other difficulties must be addressed if the research is to be ethical and to respect children as fully informed research participants.

Child-focused research not only respects children as individuals with something to say, but also enables children's perspectives and standpoints to be articulated, something which is also central to the idea of **children as researchers**. For these reasons, child-focused research is core to childhood studies, for without research of this kind, our knowledge of children's lives would be considerably impoverished.

FURTHER READING

Alderson, P. and Morrow, G. (2004) *Ethics, Social Research and Consulting with Children*. Ilford: Barnados.

Clark, A. (2010) *Transforming Children's Spaces: Children's and Adults' Participation in Designing Learning Environments*. London: Routledge.

Corsaro, W.A. and Molinari, L. (2007) 'Entering and observing in children's worlds', in P. Christensen and A. James (eds), *Conducting Research with Children* (2nd edn). London: Routledge/Falmer.

Fraser, S., Lewis, V., Ding, S., Kellet, M. and Robinson, C. (eds) (2004) *Doing Research with Children and Young People*. London: Sage.

Mandell, N. (1991) 'The least-adult role in studying children', in F.C. Waksler (ed.), *Studying the Social Worlds of Children*. London: Falmer.

Mayall, B. (2002) *Towards a Sociology of Childhood: Thinking from Children's Lives*. Buckingham: Oxford University Press.

O'Kane, C. (2007) 'The development of participatory techniques: facilitating children's views about decisions which affect them', in P. Christensen and A. James (eds), *Conducting Research with Children* (2nd edn). London: Routledge/Falmer.

Prout, A. and James, A. (1997) 'A new paradigm for the sociology of childhood: Provenance, promise and problems', in A. James and A. Prout (eds), *Constructing and Reconstructing Childhood: Contemporary Issues in the Sociological Study of Childhood* (2nd edn). London: Falmer.

Tisdall, E.K.M., Dabis, J.M. and Gallagher, M. (2009) *Researching with Children and Young People*. London: Sage.

Woodhead, M. and Faulkner, D. (2007) 'Subjects, objects or participants? Dilemmas of psychological research with children', in P. Christensen and A. James (eds), *Conducting Research with Children* (2nd edn). London: Routledge/Falmer.

key concepts in childhood studies

A description applied primarily to policy initiatives that claim to take into account children's interests.

Since the drawing up of the United Nations Convention on the Rights of the Child (**UNCRC**) 1989, there has been a groundswell of policy initiatives in European and US contexts that claim to be child-friendly. That is to say, policies are presented as meeting the **best interests** and **needs** of children and, through this, the suggestion is that previous initiatives have not specifically focused on children as either **citizens** or consumers. In this sense, policy directives from institutions that claim to be child-friendly would appear to be upholding children's **rights** as set out in the Convention.

One good example of a child-friendly initiative is the *Child Friendly Cities* initiative that emanates from UNICEF's Innocenti Research Centre. This initiative is committed to influencing local and national governments' planning policy to take account of children as inhabitants of cities. It encourages councils to engage children as active citizens who can, for example, take part in decisions about the cities in which they live through having a say about the direction of their future development. A child-friendly city is one in which children are protected from exploitation, abuse and violence and where there are, for example, suitable **spaces** for children to play and meet with their friends. It is also a city that meets the needs of all children and does not discriminate against some in terms of **gender**, **ethnicity** or disability.

However, there are many difficulties involved in creating services and institutions that are truly child-friendly. Moss and Petrie (2002), for example, argue that many children's services do not enable children's **agency** and **participation**. In their comparative analysis of public policy and **childhood** in the UK and Scandinavia, they argue that the idea of providing services and institutions *for* children – as commonly happens in the UK – is a top-down concept that is pre-determined by what adults think children need. To make such services and institutions as spaces for children that can meet the needs of all children and to which children themselves can contribute requires, they argue, a radical re-think of the idea of a national public policy. As Clark (2010) has shown, for example, very young children can be involved in thinking about how to make children's spaces more fitting for children's **needs** as they themselves define them.

However, the phrase 'child-friendly' has also slipped into more common parlance and may be used in contexts where a children's rights-based approach is not, in fact, being advocated. Instead, in these cases, the term 'child-friendly' may just be a reflection of the fact that adults have provided what *they* think are appropriate policies or facilities for children. In such cases, children are not being positioned as **social actors** with **agency** who can define their own needs, **welfare** and best interests. Indeed, when used, for example, to describe leisure facilities, it is often the needs of adults, rather than children, that are being met through the provision of segregated spaces for children. The provision of such child-friendly spaces may, for instance, work to calm adults' fears about children's safety and need for **protection**, or may serve to occupy children with games and **play** activities, thereby freeing up parents' time through providing some temporary relief from care-giving.

In a study of the provision of commercial birthday parties for children, McKendrick et al. argue, for example, that many of the leisure spaces which offer such facilities can be seen as serving 'a useful function for adults' through providing a safe place for children and relieving adults of the necessity to hold a party at home (2000: 113). However, they also observe that in providing a **child-focused** approach to play, such commercialised venues may serve to free children from their confinement within the home and help extend the environments in which children can participate. In this sense, they can also be seen to be meeting children's needs, albeit that some children may not have access to them for social or economic reasons.

Being child-friendly is, therefore, not simply about making places safe for children or ensuring that children have specific services. It is about recognising that children's requirements may be different – or the same – as those of adults and that the best way to assess what these are is to enable children to be involved in their design and implementation.

FURTHER READING

Christensen, P. and O'Brien, M. (eds) (2003) *Children in the City: Home, Neighbourhood and Community*. London: Falmer.

Clark, A. (2010) *Transforming Children's Spaces: Children's and Adults' Participation in Designing Learning Environments*. London: Routledge

McKendrick, J., Bradford, M.G. and Fielder, A.V. (2000) 'Time for a party! Making sense of the commercialisation of leisure space for children', in S.L. Holloway and G. Valentine (eds), *Children's Geographies*. London: Routledge.

Moss, P. and Petrie, P. (2002) *From Children's Services to Children's Spaces*. London: Routledge/Falmer.

See also: UNICEF's Innocenti Research Centre: www.childfriendlycities.

·· Childhood ··

The early part of the life-course; the institutional arrangements that separate children from adults and the structural space created by these arrangements that is occupied by children.

At its simplest, childhood is understood as the early phase of the life-course of all people in all societies. It is characterised by rapid physiological and psychological development and represents the beginning of the process of maturation to adulthood. In this sense, it is common to all children, irrespective of culture. However, as Woodhead (1996) has suggested, these biological 'facts' of growth and development are **culturally relative**; they are interpreted and understood in relation to ideas about children's **needs**, **welfare** and **best interests**, which vary between cultures. Thus, beyond children's basic needs for things such as food and water, childhood per se does not impose, necessarily, constraints upon what children can do or what they need once infancy is over.

Such views represent an alternative perspective on childhood, one which suggests that the conceptualisation and experience of childhood are not universal, but rather that they vary across time and space. Thus, for example, the historian Aries (1962) claimed that in medieval society childhood did not exist. Taking his evidence from pictures of children in art, he argued that few distinctions were made to mark out childhood as a distinctive phase of the life-course and that, when no longer babies, children participated in society much as adults did. While this radical claim has since been disputed by other historians, Aries's observations about the **social construction** of childhood were important, since they drew attention to the different ways in which childhood is experienced by children in different societies and cultures. Indeed, these differences are core to the **cultural politics of childhood** (James and James, 2004).

A second important definition of childhood relates to childhood as a social structural **space**. Qvortrup (1994) reminds us, for example, that childhood is a constant feature of the **structure** of all societies so that although children grow up and out of childhood as they develop into adults, in terms of the institutional arrangements of any society, 'childhood' remains – it is a space occupied by the next **generation**. In this sense, childhood is a universal feature of all societies, although each will separate 'children' from 'adults' in different ways. This constancy of childhood as a generational location within the social structure of any society is why Qvortrup (1994) argues that, despite cultural variation in children's experiences, the term 'childhood', rather than 'childhoods' in the plural, should be used. However, while this social space *does* remain, its historical character will change over time, shaped by, for example, changes in laws, policies and social practices. This returns us to the argument that childhood is not universal since its social, cultural and historical location will vary.

An additional dimension of the debate about the universalism or particularism of childhood relates to its **disappearance**. Postman (1983) and Elkind (1981), examining children's everyday lives in contemporary western cultures, argue that because of changes in technology and children's increased access to consumer goods, the boundaries between childhood and adulthood are dissolving and, in their view, this collapsing of the generational boundary is detrimental to children's well-being. Others, such as Buckingham (2000), dispute this claim. In his view, since childhood is of necessity defined in and through an oppositional relationship to adulthood, it is simply changing its form, rather than disappearing.

These arguments about the changing nature of childhood are further developed by Lee (2001), who explores childhood as a relational concept through the ideas of 'being' and 'becoming'. Childhood, he argues, is traditionally associated with ideas of dependency and **futurity**, with adulthood being seen as the end-point of growing up. However, according to Lee, since in the modern world 'adulthood' can never be regarded as a complete and stable state, then the distinction between mature adults and immature children is no longer useful. In an era of uncertainty about the nature of adulthood, childhood becomes a more complex and ambiguous status that cannot be characterised as a state of dependency and incompleteness as once it was.

The traditional **representation** of the relational and generational character of childhood that Lee criticises is one which encompasses the idea of childhood as the period in the life-course when children undergo the **socialisation** process as part of their preparation for future adult status. Other theorists have also challenged this idea by arguing that such a model of growing up is rather one-sided, since it neglects children's **agency** as **social actors**. This leads Corsaro (1997) to suggest that children are active interpreters of the social world. During childhood children learn about society and contribute to it through a process of what he calls **interpretive reproduction**.

'Childhood', then, is a term that glosses both the biological phase of early human development and the ways in which different societies classify and deal with this by providing institutions and services that are designed specifically for children – the incumbents of childhood. This has led some to argue (Prout, 2005) that to understand childhood fully, future researchers will have to address both its biological and social aspects and, importantly, the interconnections between these. In this sense, **childhood studies** is well placed to undertake such a task, given its interdisciplinary remit.

FURTHER READING

Aries, P. (1962) *Centuries of Childhood*. London: Jonathan Cape.

Buckingham, D. (2000) *After the Death of Childhood*. Cambridge: Polity.

Corsaro, W.A. (1997) *The Sociology of Childhood*. Thousand Oaks, CA: Pine Forge Press.

Elkind, D. (1981) *The Hurried Child: Growing Up Too Fast Too Soon*. Reading, MA: Addison Wesley.

James, A. and James, A.L. (2004) *Constructing Childhood: Theory, Policy and Social Practice*. Basingstoke: Palgrave.

Lee, N. (2001) *Childhood and Society: Growing Up in an Age of Uncertainty*. Buckingham: Open University Press.

Postman, N. (1983) *The Disappearance of Childhood*. London: Allen.

Prout, A. (2005) *The Future of Childhood*. London: Routledge/Falmer.

Qvortrup, J. (1994) 'Childhood matters: An introduction', in J. Qvortrup (ed.), *Childhood Matters*. Aldershot: Avebury.

Woodhead, M. (1996) 'In search of the rainbow: pathways to quality in large-scale programmes for young disadvantaged children', *Early Childhood Development: Practice and Reflections*, 10. The Hague: Bernard van Leer Foundation.

The use by States, or armed groups, of people below the age of 18 in the pursuit of armed conflicts.

Although current debates about child soldiers tend to focus on the use of children by armed groups, such as the Lord's Resistence Army, in various African conflicts, the involvement of children (as defined by the UNCRC – i.e. people below the age of 18) in war is not a new, or even a recent, phenomenon. Rosen (2005) argues that children have always been involved in fighting wars including, for example, the American Civil War. In addition, children have also always had experience of war, even if not directly involved as combatants, with, in some instances, children being specifically targeted (Wells, 2009).

Article 38 of the United Nations Convention on the Rights of the Child (**UNCRC**) 1989 requires States Parties to 'take all feasible measures to ensure that persons who have not attained the age of 15 years do not take a direct part in hostilities', requiring them to 'refrain from recruiting any person who has not attained the age of fifteen years into their armed forces'. It should be noted, however, that the latter more demanding requirements are only part of an Optional Protocol, which States Parties are not required to accept when ratifying their adoption of the UNCRC and that many have not done so, meaning that children continue to be recruited as soldiers. However, despite the apparent limitations of the UNCRC in not being able to restrict the recruitment of child soldiers, two other international criminal institutions have been established to pursue and prosecute those involved in the war crime of child recruitment: the Sierra Leone Special Court and the International Criminal Court, established in 2002. The International Criminal Court was set up under the provisions of the Rome Statute of the International Criminal Court, 1998, which has now been ratified by 111 States.

One of the many complex problems raised by the phenomenon of children who commit acts of violence in the contexts of armed conflict revolves around the question of **responsibility** – the extent to which children are, and should be, criminally responsible for such acts. This problem is particularly acute since many child soldiers are forcibly recruited to take part in armed conflicts, and although they have frequently been involved in appalling acts of violence, often against women and other children, many of them are also victims themselves. Indeed, they have often been forced to carry out such acts in very difficult circumstances and under enormous pressure, often being supplied with and under the influence of drugs and/or alcohol by those who recruit them. Thus, although there have been no criminal prosecutions of children in international tribunals, and there is general acceptance of the presumption that a child below the age of 12 should not be held

child soldiers

criminally responsible for war crimes and crimes against humanity, some domestic jurisdictions have prosecuted and even executed former child soldiers.

A further problem for **childhood studies** arises from the need to take full and proper account of children's **agency**. As Wells (2009) notes, in the African context, for example, there has always been a traditional culture of militarism for young males – they were expected to learn how to fight, and did so. It is important to acknowledge, therefore, that children are not just the passive victims of war, a view based on predominantly western understandings of childhood **innocence**. There are a range of other reasons too why children might choose to participate, the main ones being: 'to escape poverty, to secure protection, to enact revenge and for political and ideological reasons' (Wells, 2009: 152). Enlisting as soldiers, in this sense, can offer children some kind of **protection**, for girls as well as boys. However, when girls enlist or are forcibly conscripted into armies they are likely to be raped and made into 'combat wives', although this identity is one that some girls, especially those with children, may choose to adopt even after the conflict has ended. For many children, however, the process of reintegration into society may be far more difficult, although approaches that focus on developing community **resilience** (fostering better health, providing education and creating opportunities to make a livelihood) appear to offer good outcomes, albeit that the success of such projects is often hampered by the absence of long-term funding and other resources (Wessells, 2011).

FURTHER READING

Boyden, J. and de Berry, J. (eds) (2004) 'Children and youth on the front line', *Studies in Forced Migration*, Vol. 14. New York: Berghahn Books.

Briggs, J. (2005) *Innocents Lost: When Child Soldiers Go to War*. New York: Basic Books.

Gates, S. and Reich, S. (eds) (2009) *Child Soldiers in the Age of Fractured States*. Pittsburgh, PA: Pittsburgh University Press.

Rosen, D.M. (2005) *Armies of the Young: Child Soldiers in War and Terrorism*. New Brunswick, NJ: Rutgers University Press.

Wells, K. (2009) *Childhood in a Global Perspective*. Cambridge: Polity.

Wessells, M. (2011) 'The reintegration of formerly recruited girls: a resilience approach', in D.T. Cook and J. Wall (eds), *Children and Armed Conflict: Cross-disciplinary Investigations*. Basingstoke: Palgrave Macmillan.

Childhood Studies

The interdisciplinary study of the early period of the human life-course that is legally recognised and socially (as well as, in part, scientifically) defined as childhood, as distinct from adulthood.

Everybody 'knows' what a **child** and **childhood** are, because we have all been children and experienced childhood and because, as adults, we are surrounded by children living their childhoods in which, as adults, we are both participants and observers. These concepts are also a key component of social organisation and social structure, particularly in terms of **generation** and inter-generational relationships but also because of the significance of **age** in the allocation of resources and responsibilities in all cultures and societies. As discussed elsewhere in this volume, these concepts are complex and problematic; they are also, however, central to defining and understanding what we mean by childhood studies.

The beginning of this period is easy enough to define since the life-course begins at birth, although childhood studies have, with few very exceptions (see, for example, Alderson, 2000), focused their attention on slightly later stages in the life-course, when children begin to demonstrate their agency in a more readily observable way. Partly because of this, the earliest stages in the life-course – babyhood – have tended to be studied mainly by those interested in child development and early years education.

The point at which childhood ends and adulthood begins is, however, far more problematic, as our discussions of the child and childhood reveal, since this is far more a matter of social, socio-legal, historical and cultural construction. As a consequence, the stage in the life-course that borders childhood and adulthood, and which therefore marks the boundary between childhood studies and the study of subsequent stages in the life-course, is inherently problematic. By the same token, it also makes it of particular interest in the context of childhood studies since it brings into sharp focus the issue of childhood as a **social construction**.

In between these two boundaries lies the area of childhood studies, a field of study that addresses childhood as a complex social phenomenon. And precisely because of its complexity, a comprehensive understanding of childhood cannot be achieved by applying any single epistemological or disciplinary perspective: complex phenomena require interdisciplinary study, so the study of childhood must be understood as a multi- and interdisciplinary activity.

Some of the most significant contributions to the field have come from history, which has increased our understanding of the **cultural relativity** of childhood through exploring the ways in which childhoods have differed between various historical periods. Biology, medicine and psychology have made crucial contributions in terms of our understanding of the development of the child's body, brain and mind. Social psychology has offered us insights into the development of children's social attitudes, behaviours and relationships. Social policy has shed light upon the way in which policies in relation to children and families have been developed and implemented, and the models of childhood that have underpinned these developments. The disciplines of law and sociolegal studies have helped us to understand legal definitions and regulation of the child and the **family**. And yet other disciplines such as geography, education and increasingly the humanities (e.g. literature, the arts and philosophy) have brought their particular epistemologies to bear on the study and understanding of childhood. Indeed, children's geographies is now establishing itself as a distinct sub-discipline alongside, for example, a growing interest in the history of childhood.

The key conceptual and analytical catalyst, however, which was largely responsible for pulling together and exploiting the synergy between these different disciplinary perspectives initially, came from within sociology and social anthropology. Out of this, the 'new' paradigm of the social study of childhood emerged in the 1970s–1990s (James and Prout, 1990). This is partly because at the heart of sociological endeavour is the study of the relationship between social **structure** and the **agency** of individual **social actors**. Hitherto, this tension had been explored almost entirely in relation to adults. What childhood studies achieved, through both its theoretical and empirical contributions to the debate, was to demonstrate the agency of children as social actors. This firmly established the importance of embracing children as social subjects, rather than as just objects of social practices, or as empty vessels whose development was controlled purely by biological and psychological processes. As a corollary, this sociological approach also played a foundational role in another key feature of the growth of childhood studies: that is, the development of innovatory research methods which involved the active engagement of children and their participation in the research process in **child-focused research** and also seeing **children as researchers** themselves.

FURTHER READING

Alderson, P. (2000) *Young Children's Rights: Exploring Beliefs, Principles and Practice (Children in Charge)*. London: Jessica Kingsley.

Hendrick, H. (1997) *Children, Childhood and English Society 1880–1990*. Cambridge: Cambridge University Press.

Heywood, C. (2001) *A History of Childhood*. Cambridge: Polity.

Holloway, S.L. and Valentine, G. (eds) (2000) *Children's Geographies: Playing, Living, Learning*. London: Routledge.

James, A. and James, A.L. (2004) *Constructing Childhood: Theory, Policy and Social Practice*. London: Palgrave Macmillan.

James, A. and Prout, A. (eds) (1990) *Constructing and Reconstructing Childhood*. London: Falmer.

James, A., Jenks, C. and Prout, A. (1998) *Theorising Childhood*. Cambridge: Polity.

James, A.L. (2010) 'Competition or integration? The next step in childhood studies?', *Childhood*, 17(4), 485–99.

Kehily, M.J. (2004) *An Introduction to Childhood Studies*. Maidenhead: Open University Press.

Lesnik-Oberstein, K. (2011) *Children in Culture, Revisited: Further Approaches to Childhood*. Basingstoke: PalgraveMacmillan.

Prout, A. (2005) *The Future of Childhood*. London: Routledge/Falmer.

Qvortrup, J., Corsaro, W. and Honig, M. (eds) *The Palgrave Handbook of Childhood Studies*. Basingstoke: Palgrave Macmillan.

Woodhead, M. and Montgomery, H. (eds) (2003) *Understanding Childhood: An Interdisciplinary Approach*. Buckingham: Open University/ Wiley.

key concepts in childhood studies

Children as Consumers

> The act of consuming; the actions of children as consumers.

Although often considered to be a relatively new phenomenon, children have been seen as consumers ever since the development of a specific culture of children's toys and games in the 18th century. However, it was during the 19th century that the potential of children as a consumer group in society began to be fully realised. As Buckingham (2011) notes, at first this was through their parents' desire to buy into particular childhood ideals by purchasing children's toys (Cross, 1997). Later, advertisers began directing their attention to children themselves, building on the idea that children might be empowered as active consumers.

Reactions to the idea of children as consumers have become, however, increasingly ambivalent in the 21st century. On the one hand, it embraces the notion that children are **social actors**, people who are able to make choices and decisions; on the other, it provokes suspicion, by adults, that children are simply being exploited by marketing strategies that they do not recognise or understand, and over which they have little control. This has led to widespread concerns about the loss of childhood **innocence**. However, Buckingham (2011) argues that this emotionally charged and polarised debate about 'toxic' childhood is unhelpful for understanding what is actually taking place in contemporary childhood. He suggests that children's relationship to consumption has to be understood in a more nuanced and complex way.

First, Buckingham argues that the consumption practices of children need to be seen as part of their normal, everyday lives – and increasingly so, given the rapid growth of the child consumer market. Second, he suggests that attention needs to be given to the ways in which ideas of 'the child' and 'childhood' are marketed to children as well as to adults: that the 'multiple identities of the child consumer are not simply a creation of the market, but also identities that children themselves are actively constructing and performing in their everyday lives' (Buckingham, 2011: 63). Third, Buckingham argues, children are embedded within cultures of consumption that both constrain and help create children's and adults' consumption practices. Thus, for example, in their research, Russel and Tylor (2002) show how girls' practices of consumption of 'girly' artifacts have to be understood in terms of a complex interplay between the role of markets, cultural ideas of gender, and the girls' own forms of self-expression about what it is to be a girl. What research within **childhood studies** offers, then, is a challenge to many contemporary populist concerns about 'toxic' childhood and the **sexualisation** of children. Through empirically grounded studies, research shows the subtleties of the ways in which children engage with the world of consumption.

For this reason Cook (2010) argues that the concept of consumer enculturation, rather than socialisation, is more helpful. It focuses our understanding on how children learn to become consumers, rather than assuming this to be a passive, linear and gradual socialisation of this capacity in all children. Cook wants also to draw attention to the **diversity** of childhood by revealing the 'multiple trajectories of children's participation in the world of goods and meanings' (2010: 76). This enables the differences wrought by gender, class and ethnicity to be acknowledged as core to children's subjective engagement with the commercial world, as well as the fact that not all children are equally able, or wanting to, participate in the commercial world in the same way.

FURTHER READING

Buckingham, D. (2011) *The Material Child: Growing up in Consumer Culture*. Cambridge: Polity.

Buckingham, D. and Tingstad, V. (eds) (2010) *Childhood and Consumer Culture*. Basingstoke: Palgrave Macmillan.

Cook, D.T. (2010) 'Commercial enculturation: Moving beyond consumer socialization', in D. Buckingham and V. Tingstad (eds), *Childhood and Consumer Culture*. Basingstoke: Palgrave Macmillan

Cross, G. (1997) *Kids' Stuff: Toys and the Changing World of American Childhood*. Cambridge, MA: Harvard University Press.

Russel, R. and Tylor, M. (2002) 'Thank heaven for little girls: "Girl heaven" and the commercial context of feminine childhood', *Sociology*, 36(3): 619–37.

Children as Researchers

Children who carry out their own research on children and young people

Ever since the development of **childhood studies**, a commitment to carrying out **child-focused research** has been seen as a central priority, and researchers have developed a range of techniques for working with children that enable children's views and opinions to be expressed. However, with increasing recognition of the importance of children's **rights** and **participation**, some researchers have begun to explore ways in which children might carry out their own research and become researchers themselves.

The rationale for this is that, even with the adoption of child-focused research, adults' views and opinions may still come to dominate in the research process. For example, in most research projects adults choose the research topic and approach children to ask them to participate; adults decide on the methods to be adopted and, most often, remain in charge of the ensuing interpretation and writing-up of the research findings. For some researchers, such an approach to research with children goes against the spirit of the United Nations Convention on the Rights of the

Child (**UNCRC**) 1989, especially in relation to the rights of children to participate. They have argued, therefore, that children can and should be researchers in projects that seek out children's views. As Alderson puts it, 'if children's social relations and cultures are worthy of study in their own right, then who is better qualified to research some aspects of their lives than children themselves?' (2008: 278).

In arguing for children to be considered as researchers Alderson points out that, in schools, children are often already acting as researchers in relation to their school work, finding out and processing information. They therefore already have a range of research skills and some experience of the research process and, indeed, they may be willing to ask more critical questions than adults! However, the ways in which, in practice, children are considered to be researchers can embrace different levels of involvement for them at different stages in the research process. Thus, for example, in some projects children may just help adults decide the research questions; in other projects, children may generate their own questions. Similarly, children may participate by collecting their own data or be seen by adults simply as people with whom data can be generated. Alderson warns, therefore, that the kinds of participation children end up having in research can vary extensively, and that children may feel disempowered rather than empowered by their participation in research.

Listing the range of obstacles that children as researchers face, Kellet (2006) suggests that their lack of knowledge, skills and **competence** is often cited, with these lacks being seen as linked to **age and maturity**. However, as Clark (2004) showed in her work, even very young children can be actively involved as researchers; for example, by being given cameras to take photographs of things that are important to them. Indeed, Kellet argues, when given appropriate training, children can become effective researchers who can 'draw up their own research agendas ... investigate issues that they determine are important in their lives and give voice to these issues through dissemination' (2006: 332). In an article written jointly by herself as an academic and the children who carried out the research, Kellet and her co-authors show how children can become active researchers who are able to design and lead their own projects (Kellet, 2006). She concludes that this can be an empowering experience for the children.

There are, however, a number of practical and ethical issues that arise when children are researchers, which parallel many of the issues that arise more generally in relation to children's **participation** (Sinclair, 2004). For example, what level of responsibility should a child have in any particular project; should children be paid; which children get to take part; who has control over the data produced? Mason (2002), for example, highlights the need for children to be treated as employees, protected by the rules governing hours of work, and suggests that the safety of children, both physical and psychological, also has to be considered, just as it should be with adult researchers. It can also be the case that only the most articulate children get to act as researchers, leading, potentially, to a sense of disenfranchisement for those in a group who are not able to take such a direct part.

While the arguments outlined above clearly demonstrate the case for recognising children's capacities and abilities to carry out research, and also the ways in which children can be full participants in the research process rather than simply acting as research informants, as Davis has argued 'most participatory research also involves adults' who take on a variety of roles (2009: 163). In this respect James (2007) sounds a note of caution for **childhood studies** more generally. She argues that the movement towards seeing children as researchers has to be seen as part of a wider political struggle about children's **participation** and their **right** to be heard: it is not just concerned with improving research methodologies so that children's perspectives on the world can be more easily and reliably accessed. Thus, as James suggests, positioning children as researchers into their own lives does not *automatically* guarantee a more authentic or accurate account of those lives. It may do, but equally it may not. As with all research, whether carried out by children themselves or by adults on children's behalf, it remains subject to the politics of the representation process.

FURTHER READING

Alderson, P. (2008) 'Children as researchers: Participation rights and research methods', in P. Christensen and A. James (eds), *Research With Children* (2nd edn). London: Routledge.

Clark, A. (2004) 'The mosaic approach and research with young children', in V. Lewis, M. Kellett, C. Robinson, S. Fraser and S. Ding (eds), *The Reality of Research with Children and Young People*. London: Sage.

Davis, J. (2009) 'Involving children', in E.K.M. Tisdall, J.M. Davis and M. Gallagher (eds), *Researching with Children and Young People: Research Design, Methods and Analysis*. London: Sage.

James, A. (2007) 'Giving voice to children's voices: Practices and problems, pitfalls and potentials', *American Anthropologist*, 109(2): 261–72.

Kellet, M. (2006) '"Just teach us the skills please, we'll do the rest": Empowering ten-year-olds as active researchers', *Children and Society*, 18: 329–43.

Mason, J. (2000) 'Researching children's perspectives: Legal issues', in A. Lewis and G. Lindsay (eds), *Researching Children's Perspectives*. Buckingham: Open University Press.

Sinclair, R. (2004) 'Participation in practice', *Children & Society*, 18(2): 106–18.

Children's Voices

> *In the context of research and public policy, calls for children's voices to be heard refers to the process of allowing children to articulate their views on matters that concern them.*

The development of a new paradigm for the study of children within the social sciences in the 1970s (Prout and James, 1990) called for children and young people to be recognised as **social actors** and for their views and perspectives to be heard in order that their position in society might be better understood. Hardman (1973) suggested that children were literally 'muted' because their perspectives on society were not heard by adults; indeed, adults occupying positions of power and authority over children often silenced them. Since that time, this call for children to be able to articulate their views has extended beyond the confines of the academic world, following the almost universal ratification of the United Nations Convention on the Rights of the Child (**UNCRC**) in 1989. Having access to the views and interests of children and young people is now acknowledged as important by governments across the world for the development of policy initiatives around **childhood** and **youth**. Accessing the views and voices of children is also a significant feature of the ways in which many non-governmental organisations involved in the promotion of child **welfare** and children's **rights** now carry out and disseminate their work.

Prior to the 1970s, however, what children had to say about their position in society was not given much prominence, either in academic research or in relation to public policy. Although in the USA, anthropologists such as Margaret Mead (1928) and Ruth Benedict (1935) had been working directly with children, their interest was in how children acquire particular cultural traits during the **socialisation** process and the effects these have on personality development. Only later through, for example, the anthropological work of Bluebond-Langner (1978), did it become apparent that what children had to say about their experiences as children might offer a rather different perspective on the social world. What Bluebond-Langner's research revealed was that children who were dying of cancer often knew their prognosis, despite parents and doctors attempting to hide it from them. Through conversations with children, she was able to show how the children participated in a form of mutual pretence by not revealing to the adults who cared for them that they were aware of the progression of their illness.

In contemporary childhood research, however, it is now commonplace for researchers to adopt **child-focused research** methods and to talk directly with children and young people in order to ascertain their views and perspectives. When reporting their work, these researchers invariably include in the text direct quotations from what children tell them. It is important to remember, however, that these children's voices, represented by quotations taken from children, have been chosen by the researcher or writer. In this sense, they may have been selected specifically to illustrate a particular argument or to present a point of view. As in any piece of reporting, therefore, these voices are not unmediated. It is important that readers pay attention to how and why children's words are being incorporated in an article or document and what this **representation** of childhood accomplishes, since children's voices, in this sense, are often textually mediated.

In the policy field this is a particular problem for, following the UNCRC, and especially Article 12, which says that children should be consulted about matters that concern them, many governments and organisations are now attempting to consult with children and to represent their views. However, in some cases, the process of consultation may be rather limited, with only lip-service being paid to what children say seriously (see, for example, James and James, 2008). Indeed, as Morgan (2005) notes, although numerous organisations may now consult with children, rather fewer feed back to them and fewer still make their views count. This suggests that recognition of the importance of getting children's voices heard, and acknowledging children and young people's participation as **citizens** with ideas to contribute *as children*, remains rather patchy. Roberts, for instance, writing about the policy field in the UK, argues that although children are now being more involved in decisions that affect their lives, 'it cannot be taken for granted that more listening means more hearing' (2008: 264). Indeed, Smart (2002) argues that, despite the eagerness shown, for example, by the family law system to embrace children's voices in divorce proceedings, the complex accounts that children provide are often difficult to accommodate. Just because children's voices are represented, therefore, this does not mean that their views and opinions will be taken notice of.

More recently, however, there has been a move within **childhood studies** to see **children as researchers** themselves and to carry out their own research into subjects that are pertinent to their everyday lives (Jones, 2004). As part of the children's rights agenda (Alderson, 2007), this **participation** by children as co-researchers, or even sole researchers, is often regarded as one way to avoid the problems of tokenism that can arise when trying to include children's voices in research or policy initiatives.

One final problem is raised by the concept of children's voices. Often, the inclusion of 'the voice of the child' is cited as a goal of policy development, an aim made explicit in, and necessary because of, the provisions of Article 12 of the UNCRC, the overall aim of which is to promote the **best interests** of 'the child'. Here, even though children are the focus of concern, they are conceptually categorised together in the context of their collective **vulnerability**, under a single label, as if their **needs** and best interests can be articulated with one largely undifferentiated voice, irrespective of class or culture. Doing this runs the risk, therefore, that far from giving children greater audibility and visibility in their different **social worlds**, children are simply further disempowered and their voices rendered silent once more by adult determination of what their needs are, what is in their best interests, and what constitutes their welfare. It may also mean that only the more audible children's voices get heard; for example, those who are poor or who are disabled may find fewer opportunities to express their views.

FURTHER READING

Alderson, P. (2007) 'Children as researchers: The effects of participation rights on research methodology', in P. Christensen and A. James (eds), *Research with Children* (2nd edn). London: Falmer.

Benedict, R. (1935) *Patterns of Culture*. London: Routledge & Kegan Paul.

Bluebond-Langner, M. (1978) *The Private Worlds of Dying Children*. Princeton, NJ: Princeton University Press.

Hardman, C. (1973) 'Can there be an anthropology of children?', *Journal of the Anthropology Society of Oxford*, 4(1): 85–99.

James, A.L. and James, A. (2008) 'Changing childhood in the UK: Reconstructing discourses of "risk" and "protection"', in A. James and A.L. James (eds), *European Childhoods: Cultures, Politics and Childhoods in Europe*. London: Palgrave.

Jones, A. (2004) 'Involving children and young people as researchers', in S. Fraser, V. Lewis, S. Ding, M. Kellet and C. Robinson (eds), *Doing Research with Children and Young People*. London: Sage.

Mead, M. (1928) *Coming of Age in Samoa*. Harmondsworth: Penguin.

Morgan, R. (2005) 'Finding what children say they want: Messages from children', *Representing Children*, 17(3): 180–89.

Prout, A. and James, A. (1990) 'A new paradigm for the sociology of childhood? Provenance, promise and problems', in A. James and A. Prout (eds), *Constructing and Reconstructing Childhood*. Basingstoke: Falmer.

Roberts, H. (2008) 'Listening to children: And hearing them', in P. Christensen and A. James (eds), *Research with Children* (2nd edn). London: Falmer.

Smart, C. (2002) 'From children's shoes to children's voices', *Family Court Review*, 40: 307–19.

Citizenship

> *A status that is given to members of a community who share those rights, respon-sibilities, duties and adopt those social practices that are intrinsic to belonging to and being a responsible member of that community and who, in return, share in the resources that are distributed within that community.*

Defining citizenship is far from easy. This is not least because by the act of defining it, valuable economic and political rights and valued social status are allocated. Indeed, one of the traditional sanctions for ignoring the responsibilities and duties attached to citizenship is the withdrawal of some or all components of that status; for example, historically through exile, or through the loss of voting rights for those imprisoned for criminal offences. Given the importance of citizenship status, therefore, it is hardly surprising that definitions of citizenship are highly contested. In essence, they reflect a variety of different social and political positions in relation to what constitutes community membership and what rights and obligations are associated with such membership. And as a consequence, these different perspectives determine issues of social inclusion and exclusion.

Also embedded in most definitions of citizenship are notions of independence, **maturity**, **competence** and belonging; that is, a citizen is one who has the moral and practical ability to exercise the **rights** and discharge the responsibilities and duties of citizenship responsibly. Thus, citizens who belong to a community are expected to be independent, mature and competent enough to contribute fully to the life of that community and, in turn, to receive a share of its resources. It is hardly surprising, then, if citizenship is intrinsically such a complex and contested issue, that the issue of determining children's citizenship status should be even more difficult. Indeed, in his seminal analysis of citizenship, Marshall (1950) did not regard children as citizens, since they are dependent upon adults and have no political rights; for him, children could only be regarded as citizens in waiting.

Given the widespread view in western industrialised societies (in which the economic and educational dependence of children has become ever more protracted) that children lack competence, it is perhaps unsurprising that they should be denied the status of citizens. Such a view is buttressed by the pervasive influence of **developmental psychology**, which serves to emphasise children's lack of moral competence and their developmental incompleteness when compared to adults. The status of citizenship is therefore reserved for those who are fully competent and responsible members of the community (i.e. adults) even though it is questionable whether the behaviour and decision-making ability of some adults are markedly different from that of some children!

Such a view of children is, historically, fairly recent in western industrialised countries. Indeed, Cockburn (1998) argues that the exclusion of children from full community membership and the denial of their status as citizens only became firmly institutionalised during the 19th century. This was a period in which there was a rapid expansion of social policies that were designed to remove children from areas of adult and public life and to segregate them in **schools** under the guise of education and protection (Hendrick, 1997). It was therefore a process that went hand-in-hand with the growth of modern conceptions of **childhood** and children's **welfare**. However, these 'progressive', welfare-based policies set children apart from the public world and **space** of adults, establishing the foundations for the **age**-based social exclusion of children from full membership of the community and therefore from citizenship.

Citizenship is an unfolding process that cannot simply be switched on at some arbitrary point in a child's life. And while it might be difficult to talk about citizenship and rights in relation to a 9-month-old child, the position of a 16-year-old child is very different. It is therefore important to consider whether it is sufficient to treat children purely as citizens of the future, and also to consider the extent to which such issues are historically and **culturally relative**.

Crucially, however, we must reflect on the extent to which we can talk realistically of children's rights if children are not citizens (Lister, 2007). Certainly it might be argued that their **participation** rights under the United Nations Convention on the Rights of the Child (**UNCRC**) 1989 are a symbolic **representation** of and an attempt to enhance their citizenship status. Participation does not equal citizenship, however, since this is rooted in a social, political and therefore legal identity that is only conferred upon adults, as bearers of rights and full members of the community. Only the citizen can, as an autonomous legal entity, seek to assert their rights on their own behalf. The legal identity and dependence of children mean that, in most respects and in most societies, they are dependent upon the State or upon individual adults to assert, or to seek to secure or enforce their rights, be these rights relating to welfare, **protection**, provision or participation.

We must therefore be aware that the rights contained in the UNCRC constitute human rights articulated specifically in relation to children. As such, they represent ethical or moral rights rather than legally enforceable citizenship rights. Thus it can be argued that, somewhat perversely, because children's rights as currently constructed are not rooted in the social and legal status of citizenship, they serve to reinforce children's dependence on adults.

FURTHER READING

Cockburn, T. (1998) 'Children and citizenship in Britain', *Childhood*, 5(1): 99–117.

Hendrick, H. (1997) 'Constructions and reconstructions of British childhood: An interpretive survey, 1800 to the present', in A. James and A. Prout (eds), *Constructing and Reconstructing Childhood: Contemporary Issues in the Sociological Study of Childhood* (2nd edn). London: Falmer.

Invernizzi, A. and Williams, J. (eds.) *Children and Citizenship*. London: Sage.

Kjørholt, A.T. (2002) 'Small is powerful: Discourses on "children and participation" in Norway', *Childhood*, 9(1): 63–82.

Kjørholt, A.T. (2005) 'The competent child and the "right to be oneself": Reflections on children as fellow citizens in a day-care centre', in A. Clark, A.T. Kjørholt and P. Moss (eds), *Beyond Listening*. Bristol: The Policy Press.

Lister, R. (2007) 'Why citizenship: Where, when and how children?' *Theoretical Inquiries in Law*, 8(2): 693–718.

Marshall, T.H. (1950) *Citizenship and Social Change*. London: Pluto.

Turner, B.S. (ed.) (1993) *Citizenship and Social Theory*. London: Sage.

Competence

competence

> *The ability, capacity or qualification to perform a task, fulfil a function or to meet the requirements of a role to an acceptable standard.*

The notion of competence is not inherently complicated and although some of its specific meanings are more nuanced (e.g. that of legal competence, which may be used to define legal status or authority) and it has acquired a particular currency in recent years in terms of the specification of the detailed components of a skill, the basic meaning is as defined above: that is, the ability to 'do' something. In this performative sense, it should be noted that competence does not even necessarily have to be defined in terms of the quality of a given performance. Indeed, the use of the term to describe the performance of a given task may be intended to imply that it was no more than adequate in terms of meeting the required standard – it was 'competent', rather than 'excellent' or even 'good'.

These may seem fine points of semantic detail and usage but they acquire a particular significance in the context of **childhood studies** and debates about children's competence. In this context, competence is regarded by many adults as being intimately linked to chronological **age**. This is as a result of the paradigm of children's development offered by **developmental psychology**, implicit in which is an emphasis on children's relative *in*competence, immaturity and dependency. This still exercises a powerful influence over adult perceptions of children and their abilities and freedom to act, for the assessment of competence is closely associated with the allocation of **responsibility**.

In the light of the definition used here, it must be acknowledged, however, that the notion of competence is **culturally relative** and spans a wide range of attributes, including physical, cognitive, emotional, social and moral capacities. Such qualities do not develop uniformly, either in terms of chronology or of cultural context. As cross-cultural comparisons make abundantly clear, children cannot be viewed as a homogeneous group, since their abilities and levels of functioning at any given age are far from universal. Where different assumptions about competence are made and applied, as inevitably happens in different cultures, different behaviours and practices arise. A good illustration of this is **working children** in the majority South, who may perform many activities that, in other contexts, might be regarded as impossible for children to carry out effectively.

In making such judgements, age is frequently used as a proxy for competence – in other words, children's abilities and the responsibilities they are given are determined not on the basis of their abilities or competence but on the basis of their chronological age. This happens even though such age-based determination of competence ceases once adulthood has been achieved and in spite of the fact that competence is something dynamic. It develops on the basis of increased opportunities for participation and the confidence achieved through such experiences, throughout an individual's life-course.

Such linkages between age and competence continue to be made, despite the fact that there is now a substantial body of research clearly demonstrating that there is no necessary link and that even young children can be morally competent, capable of making informed and morally valid decisions, and may even demonstrate a greater capacity to do so than some adults. Another spurious connection that is sometimes made is between competence and intelligence, but there is no evidence that intelligent children are necessarily more competent. Neither is there evidence to suggest that having a sheltered or disadvantaged background necessarily has any links to competence – disadvantaged children are no more and no less competent than those from sheltered backgrounds.

There are also few innate limits on children's competence. In other words, the failure of adults to give children **responsibility** can limit their ability to learn how to become competent and to develop their competences (i.e. skills). Conversely, if children are given responsibility and, if necessary, guidance, they frequently demonstrate levels of competence much higher than many adults might anticipate: children learn by experience and competence grows through experience, rather than simply with age.

This view is reinforced by a recent review of research into children's own perspectives and experiences by Lansdown (2005). This concluded that adults consistently under-estimate children's capacities and that, as a consequence, children are denied opportunities for participation in decision making and the exercise of responsibility in many areas of their lives. In many affluent countries, this is at least in part because of the extended period of social and economic dependency associated with **childhood** and, connected with this, an enhanced perception of the need for child **protection** during this period. Evidence suggests that this is also because the assessment of children's levels of competence often relies on methods that serve to inhibit rather than demonstrate their level of understanding. As Lansdown (2005) argues, the development of **child-friendly** tests is essential if a more informed understanding of their competence is to be achieved.

Because of its association with responsibility, competence is also linked with arguments about the **citizenship** status of children and their **rights**. These are, of course, intimately linked with the age at which children are deemed to cease to be children and to have become adults. In this context, children who have not reached the age of majority are not deemed to be competent to exercise the political and social responsibilities required of citizens, for example.

A key challenge for childhood studies is therefore to make clear the distinction between age and competence and to make sure the latter is appropriately assessed. This might involve, for example, the direct assessment of a child's competence to perform a specific task or discharge a particular function, rather than assuming their incompetence on the basis of age. The movement towards seeing **children as researchers**, for example, works with such a model of competence (Danby and Farrel, 2004), but a more radical change, as Lansdown suggests, would be to introduce a presumption of competence in the exercise of rights, placing the onus on adults to demonstrate a child's incapacity in any particular context, in order to restrict their exercise of rights (2005: 50).

competence

FURTHER READING

Alderson, P. (2000) *Young Children's Rights: Exploring Beliefs, Principles and Practice*. London: Jessica Kingsley.

Danby, S. and Farrel, A. (2004) 'Accounting for young children's competence in educational research: New perspectives in research ethics', *Australian Educational Researcher*, 31(3): 35–49.

Hutchby, I. and Moran-Ellis, J. (1997) *Children and Social Competence*. London: Falmer.

Lansdown, G. (2005) *The Evolving Capacities of the Child*. Florence: UNICEF Innocenti Research Centre/Save the Children.

Cultural Politics of Childhood

> The cultural politics of childhood refers to the combination of national and therefore cultural contexts, social practices and political processes through which childhood is uniquely constructed in different societies at different times.

In arguing that **childhood** is a **social construction** and that there is no such thing as a single childhood, rather a multiplicity of childhoods, the interdisciplinary approach to the understanding of childhood has coalesced around the label of 'childhood studies'. In the process, however, it has had to engage with the thorny issue of how so many different childhoods are produced and sustained, particularly in the context of the pressures generated by the growth of discourses about the globalisation of childhood and children's **rights** in the wake of the United Nations Convention on the Rights of the Child (**UNCRC**) 1989.

The cultural politics of childhood plays a key role in understanding this process. It does so by focusing attention on the cultural factors that determine the different images and understandings of childhood which exist in any given society at any given historical moment. Importantly, this also includes the influence children themselves can exercise over these **representations** either collectively (e.g. through the actions of school students as in Chile in 2006) or individually (e.g. through the actions of individuals such as the shootings at Columbine High in the USA or the killing of Jamie Bulger in the UK). It also includes the political mechanisms and processes, such as the framing of social policy and subsequent legislation, through which these representations of childhood are given practical expression in everyday life at any given time. Taken together, these cultural determinants, political mechanisms, and the discourses they produce, work to construct and define childhood and thereby control, or at the very least constrain, what children can actually do in any given society.

The assertion that there are a multiplicity and **diversity** of childhoods raises numerous questions, however. In what ways and under what circumstances is 'being a child' a shared and common experience? How much does the experience of 'being a child' vary, in what ways and why? Why is it that children's '**needs**' are defined and institutionalised differently, in terms of a rights agenda, in different cultural contexts and different historical eras? Why is it that, even *within* societies, the diversities in children's experiences are often masked, downplayed or regulated for the sake of emphasising commonality? What are the precise mechanisms through which childhood comes to be constituted in society in the particular form that it does, and how and why does this change?

In short, what are the precise ways in which social, economic, legal and political systems position children in any given society and culture, and what are children's and adults' responses to that positioning? The concept of the cultural politics of childhood seeks to provide a framework within which such questions can be considered by drawing attention to the dynamic, interrelated and intergenerational processes through which childhood is socially constructed. It also seeks to acknowledge the significance of the actions not only of adults but also of children themselves in the social construction of childhood and their potential as agents of social change.

In addressing these questions, this concept also helps us to understand the relationship between **structure** and **agency** (Martin and Dennis, 2010). In terms of social analysis, the idea of structure lends itself to understanding social relationships at a macro level while agency focuses on the micro level, suggesting both a rigid dichotomy and an unbridgeable conceptual gap. The relationship between these twin pillars of social and cultural reproduction is not fixed, however – rather, we need to understand it as dynamic. In order to understand this interrelationship, we must re-think the notion of social structure and the institutions through which it is constituted (such as the family and the law). Instead of seeing these as rigid forms which, as the terms suggest, constrain the individual, they might better be understood as more fluid and socially constructed contexts in which social action takes place, and through which agency is expressed and given meaning in terms of daily life. It is through this dynamic interaction that the cultural politics of childhood are shaped.

The recognition of the 'ongoing' nature of social action in the context of this dynamic interrelationship between structure and agency is central to the cultural politics of childhood because it allows us to consider both change *and* continuity as important features in the social construction and reconstruction of childhood. It also allows us to see this as being influenced by both the intentional and unintentional actions and interactions of children, as well as adults, and as a feature of **generational** relations and a wide range of other personal, social and cultural factors. This perspective thus offers a way to circumvent the either/or dichotomy of structure/agency in explaining the continuities and discontinuities of childhood, since it encourages exploration of the interactions that occur between the different elements in society in order to identify and understand the mechanisms and processes of change.

We must also acknowledge, however, the limitations of such a perspective and, in particular, the challenge posed by the universality of childhood. First, childhood does, indeed, constitute a particular biological phase in the life-course for all members of all societies. Thus, regardless of the cultural politics of childhood, children's **competences** and skills are, to some degree, shaped by the 'facts' of their ongoing physiological and psychological development. Although this takes place in, and is conditioned by, the cultural context in which it occurs, it also takes place *despite* this context. To this extent children do, indeed, share the experience of processes of maturation, regardless of the cultural framing of what constitutes maturity.

Second, we must acknowledge another shared experience of children: that eventually all children grow up and leave their 'childhood' behind them. In this sense, as Qvortrup et al. (1994) argue, 'childhood' is a constant structural feature of all societies. At the very least, therefore, while continuing to argue for a cultural politics of childhood that explains the processes by which diverse and culturally specific forms of childhood are produced, we must also acknowledge childhood as a universal feature of the life-course, which all societies deal with through the imposition of structures, laws, rules and social practices of different kinds that separate 'children' from 'adults' in one way or another. This means that amidst the diversity of childhoods produced by diverse and different cultural politics of childhood, children also have some important shared experiences and characteristics.

Although childhood as a social space *does* remain, as Qvortrup rightly argues, both a constant and a universal component of the social and structural space of each and every society, it must also be acknowledged as a matter of historical fact that the character of childhood changes over time. And it does so in ways that are specific to particular cultural contexts, in response to the shifting cultural politics of childhood – that is, as a consequence of changes in the laws, policies, discourses and social practices through which childhood is defined and within which context children exercise their agency. In this way they help shape the very processes that define the childhoods they experience and the social **space** of childhood that they eventually leave behind them.

This perspective allows us to see the individual child as a **social actor** in the collectivity of children that exists in the social space of childhood. It also allows us to recognise both the uniqueness of his/her childhood as well as its universality as a phase in the life-course. Understanding the cultural politics of childhood helps us to understand childhood as the product of the relations that adults have with children, which are also located within the broader social, political and economic frameworks that shape society's institutional arrangements (**work, schools, families**, churches, etc.) and through which children's daily lives unfold. It also helps us to understand the importance of recognising children as participants in those institutions – as part-time workers, school children, as family members and church-goers – whose actions may, in turn, have consequences for the shape that childhood takes (Thomas, 2009).

FURTHER READING

James, A. and James, A.L. (2004) *Constructing Childhood: Theory, Policy and Social Practice.* London: Palgrave Macmillan.

Martin, P.J. and Dennis, A. (2010) *Human Agents and Social Structures.* Manchester: Manchester University Press.

Qvortrup, J., Bardy, M., Sgritta, G. and Wintersberger, H. (eds) (1994) *Childhood Matters.* Aldershot: Avebury.

Scheper-Hughes, N. and Sargent, C. (eds) (1998) *Small Wars: The Cultural Politics of Childhood.* Berkeley, CA: University of California Press.

Stephens, S. (ed.) (1995) *Children and the Politics of Culture.* Princeton, NJ: Princeton University Press.

Thomas, N. (2009) *Children, Politics and Communication: Particiaption at the Margins.* Bristol: The Policy Press.

Cultural Relativism

> *The recognition that societies differ in their cultural attitudes to social phenomena and therefore no universal criteria can be applied to compare one cultural view with another. Cultures can therefore only be judged through reference to their own standards.*

The fact that in every society children are born, grow through their infancy and childhood, and eventually develop into adults might suggest that this universal experience provides the basis for shared understandings and attitudes to children – a **global** form of childhood. This is, however, not the case and evidence from societies in different parts of the world reveals a wide range of attitudes towards children and expectations of what children can or cannot do (Montgomery, 2009). For example, while in western European countries and the USA children are not permitted to marry below the age of 16, in parts of the Indian subcontinent girls may still be married at the relatively young age of 12. From a western European perspective, however, such early marriage might be reconceptualised as a form of child **sexual abuse**. A comparable example in relation to child **health** would be the practice of female circumcision. Still common in many parts of Africa, this involves the removal of the clitoris and sometimes also the labia of young girls, as a symbolic act to mark and celebrate their transition to womanhood. As Shaughnessy (1998) argues, when viewed from outside this cultural context, this traditional practice is condemned as female genital mutilation (FGM) and calls are made for its abolition. That this view is also now being increasingly voiced from within these societies reveals the complexities of some of the moral difficulties raised by the concept of cultural relativism.

Cultural relativists would argue that societies have the right to their own viewpoints and perspectives, and that such cultural practices are understandable in terms of the particular cultural contexts in which they take place. They should therefore be freed from outside interference since to do otherwise would represent an act of ethnocentrism – that is, judging another culture through the moral frames of reference of one's own **ethnicity**. Others would argue, however, that since practices such as FGM during **childhood** often cause considerable suffering and also result in poor health outcomes, a universal, rather than a culturally specific, moral code must apply and that the practice must be ended.

In the case of cultural practices that are injurious to children and young people's health and **welfare**, the argument *against* cultural relativism is easy to defend. In relation to other issues, however, cultural relativism appears less contentious and, indeed, might be deemed to help foster children's **rights** in particular cultural contexts – for example, their right to **work** or to combine work with **schooling**. This is ironic since the United Nations Convention on the Rights of the Child (**UNCRC**) 1989, although acknowledging the significance of culture in some of its

Articles, is framed in terms of the universality of its provisions, declaring a set of universal rights that are, in theory, applicable to all children across the globe.

In turn, the question of cultural relativism is also raised in relation to the increasing globalisation of the ideas that are central to the **social construction** of western childhood. As Boyden argues, while the UNCRC has in many ways achieved a great deal in terms of fostering children's rights globally, it has also helped foster a set of moral ideologies that reflect the welfare concerns of practitioners from affluent countries, which have had the 'effect of penalizing, or even criminalizing, the childhoods of the poor' (Boyden, 1997: 207). Without adequate recognition, for example, of the ways in which schooling can turn out to have negative rather than positive consequences for children living in **poverty** in the majority South, the setting of 'global standards for childhood and common policies for child welfare may be far from the enlightened step anticipated by its proponents' (Boyden, 1997: 214). In such instances, the recognition of the role that cultural relativism can play is important.

Given the huge diversity in children's lives and experiences across the world, as well as within any one society in terms of class and ethnicity for example, adopting a culturally relativist position with regard to children and childhood would seem to be appropriate. However, given children's **minority group status** in all societies, their lack of access to power and **citizenship**, and also their potential **vulnerability** to abuse and injustice from the adult world, the question arises as to whether the culturally relativist position is still a tenable one (Wells, 2009). As children are, on the whole, in need of **protection** since they are unable to defend their own interests, then surely it must behove adults to defend them on their behalf? The question is, what kind of standards are to be set?

As we have seen, the UNCRC represented an important attempt to overcome some of the limits of cultural relativism in order to ensure children's well-being worldwide, and yet it has been only partially successful: two countries – the United States and Somalia – have yet to ratify the Convention. Many countries, including the UK, entered reservations when ratifying the Convention, which enabled them, in effect, to opt out of implementing selected provisions with which they disagreed; and Africa has put in place an African Charter of Rights that is felt to reflect, more closely, the specific needs and interests of African children. Significantly, and illustrating the complexity of working with issues of cultural relativism, the Egyptian Parliament, on approving the African Children's Charter in 2001, still felt the need to reject some parts, such as the provisions relating to adoption and setting the minimum marriage age for girls at 18, as being contrary to Islamic Law and Egyptian tradition (James and James, 2004).

FURTHER READING

Boyden, J. (1997) 'Childhood and the policy makers: A comparative perspective on the globalization of childhood', in A. James and A. Prout (eds), *Constructing and Reconstructing Childhood: Contemporary Issues in the Sociological Study of Childhood*, (2nd edn). London: Falmer.

James, A. and James, A.L. (2004) *Constructing Childhood: Theory, Policy and Social Practice*. London: Palgrave Macmillan.

key concepts in
childhood studies

Montgomery, H. (2009) *An Introduction to Childhood: Anthropological Perspectives on Children's Lives*. Oxford: WileyBlackwell.

Shaughnessy, L. (1998) 'Female genital mutilation: Beyond mutilating mothers and foreign feminists', *Women's Studies Review*, 5: 123–34.

Wells, K. (2009) *Childhood in a Global Perspecticve*. Cambridge: Polity.

Woodhead, M. and Montgomery, H. (2003) *Understanding Childhood: An Interdisciplinary Approach*. Milton Keynes/Chichester: Open University/Wiley.

Delinquency

> In its broadest sense, delinquency is a term used to describe behaviour that involves a rejection or defiance of social norms or an abrogation of duty or **responsibility**. It is, however, a term that has also become specifically and indelibly associated with misbehaviour or offending in children and young people.

In the context of the UK and many other western countries, delinquency and juvenile delinquency have become almost synonymous with the commission of criminal offences by children and young people – that is, behaviours that are contrary to the criminal law. It is also the case that, drawing on its more general meaning, the term 'juvenile delinquent' is widely used to describe a child or young person who engages in petty offending or behaviour that is anti-social or generally unacceptable – that is, behaviour which defies adults' standards or expectations of what is acceptable in a child or young person.

It is important to note, however, that although European criminal justice systems may criminalise many behaviours in similar ways (e.g. property offences such as theft, or offences against the person), it would be wrong to assume that every behaviour proscribed by the criminal law in the UK, for example, is necessarily proscribed in the same form elsewhere in western Europe, let alone elsewhere in the world. This is because, as the study of the sociology of deviance has revealed, perceptions and definitions of what constitutes delinquency vary enormously according to social, cultural and historical contexts.

Central to this is the notion that there are few absolute definitions of what behaviours constitute an offence, and even fewer examples of behaviours that are universally proscribed, under all circumstances. Thus definitions of delinquency are fluid and can change, even over relatively short periods of time, and behaviours that may once have been regarded as little more than a nuisance can become criminalised. A clear illustration of this in England and Wales is the recent criminalisation of relatively low-level anti-social behaviour in the context of what is regarded by some as part of the demonisation of children and **youth**, a process that may also

delinquency

37

reflect contemporary understandings of **gender,** ethnicity and race (Alexander, 2004). This reflects a trend for the increasing regulation of various aspects of their behaviour, especially their use of public **spaces** Such shifts can be understood in terms of what the rebellious child represents in the context of the prevailing **cultural politics of childhood** – that is, a symbolic challenge to the status quo and also to adults' **representations** of childhood **innocence** (James and James, 2004).

It would also be wrong to assume that the **age** at which children and young people can be prosecuted for delinquent or criminal behaviour in the criminal courts is the same. Even in the UK there are important differences. Children aged eight and over are capable of being prosecuted in Scotland, but the equivalent age in England and Wales is ten. In France, a child under 13 is presumed to be incapable of crime and cannot be prosecuted; in Austria, Germany and Italy, the equivalent age is 14; in Norway, Sweden and Denmark, the age is 15; and in Spain and Belgium, the age is 16. The upper age – that is, the age at which a child or young person is legally deemed to be an adult and can be treated as such by the criminal justice system in terms of prosecution, trial, sentencing and sanctions – can also vary. Thus, for example, in the USA, the upper age varies, depending upon State law, between 16 and 18.

Such variations reflect significant differences in approaches to the **social construction** of childhood, differences that can have a major and long-term impact on a child's life-chances, depending in part upon international variations in the nature and severity of the sanctions used in response to delinquency (e.g. the use of custodial sentences). This is particularly important given the evidence that demonstrates that the large majority of delinquents subsequently grow out of patterns of delinquent-offending behaviour. Thus an important role of the United Nations Convention on the Rights of the Child (**UNCRC**) 1989 is its attempt to mitigate the extremes of such variations.

Such aspects of criminal behaviour apart, the meaning and definitions of what constitutes delinquency can vary enormously between different cultural contexts. Thus, for example, in the USA, children who defy parental authority in various ways – for example, through under-age alcohol consumption, truancy from school, general 'ungovernability' or 'incorrigibility' (refusal to obey parents), and running away from home – are referred to as 'status offenders'. In other words, their behaviour is outlawed solely because of their status as minors. Such behaviours can be described and dealt with as juvenile delinquency. It is dealt with by police who channel 'offenders' into a separate subsystem of group homes and shelters, where they are labelled as persons in need of supervision, children in need of **protection** and services, or minors in need of supervision by the court or child protective agency. In the UK, however, the term 'delinquency' continues to be associated primarily with relatively minor criminal behaviour by young people, and there is no comparable legal equivalent to the 'status offender'.

The debate about delinquency thus implicitly reflects broader debates about the social construction of childhood and, in particular, about the relationship between the **agency** of children: the extent to which they choose to offend (and therefore 'deserve' to be punished accordingly) versus the influence of **structure** (the extent to which factors such as class, **poverty**, **ethnicity**, gender, education or **family** determine both their behaviour and their life-chances).

FURTHER READING

Alexander, C. (2004) 'Imagining the Asian gang: Ethnicity, masculinity and youth after the "riots"', *Critical Social Policy*, 24(4): 526–49.

Downes, D. and Rock, P. (2007) *Understanding Deviance*. Oxford: Oxford University Press.

France, A. and Homel, R. (2006) 'Societal access routes and developmental pathways: Putting social structure and young people's voice into the analysis of pathways into and out of crime', *Australian and New Zealand Journal of Criminology*, 39(3): 295–309.

Frankel, S. (in press) *Children, Morality and Society*. Basingstoke: Palgrave Macmillan.

James, A. and James, A.L. (2004) *Constructing Childhood: Theory, Policy and Social Practice*. London: Palgrave Macmillan.

Maguire, M., Morgan, R. and Reiner, R. (eds) (2002) *Oxford Handbook of Criminology*. Oxford: Oxford University Press.

Developmental Psychology

The branch of psychology that has sought to define the staged and linear progression of children's cognitive and moral development in relation to their chronological age.

It is arguable that developmental psychology has, since the early 20th century, had a greater influence over our views and understanding of and attitudes towards children and **childhood** than any other single discipline. This might be explained by several factors. Developmental psychology emerged in the context of the historical development of positivism in the late 19th and early 20th centuries. This saw the social sciences attempting to emulate the scientific methods of the natural sciences in classifying, ordering, theorising and predicting the behaviour of natural phenomena. It also emerged, however, at a point in social history when children had begun to be identified as a separate social category, one that presented special problems and had special **needs** in terms of **protection** and **welfare** in comparison with adults, and thus merited special study. Hendrick (1997) refers to the emergence of the psycho-medical child and the welfare child as dominant motifs at this time, the study of the **child** as a social object consolidating around subsequent developments in medicine and psychology.

Piaget became one of the leading authorities on the psychological development of children. Drawing on his research, in 1950 he published (in *The Psychology of Intelligence*) what was then the definitive version of the cognitive development of children. In this he described them as initially egocentric and only gradually developing their moral sensibilities and achieving powers of reasoning that comply with expectations for rational adult thinking. Importantly, he described both children's cognitive and moral development in a highly deterministic way: as a series of discrete stages, each defined in terms of a specific cognitive structure, the achievement of each being necessary before moving on to the next. In essence he argued that, for all children everywhere, there is staged and linear progression to adulthood, central to which was his view of children's inherent lack of skills and their subsequent acquisition of these through clearly defined stages, linked to clearly specified ages.

Thus in Piaget's schema, **age** and **competence** are thoroughly intertwined: the developing child is determined by its developing body and thus childhood came to be seen as the epitome of the lack of competence, while adulthood is the model of competence. This necessarily defined children as social objects, rather than as social subjects possessed of **agency**, and as being 'en route' – in the process of becoming adults rather than being children.

Piaget's ideas, as well as those of others who followed in his footsteps, such as Kohlberg, were buttressed by biological determinism, the biological/medical view of children's development that also encourages us to focus on the relationship between chronological age and various kinds of physical qualities and attributes, rather than the competence of individual children.

There is little doubt that as, arguably, the founding father of developmental psychology, Piaget influenced subsequent generations of psychologists with his theories about cognitive and moral development. More importantly, his ideas reached well beyond the academic world and also influenced the thinking of a great many adults and parents. The reach and impact of his thinking can be understood further by recognising the power of and widespread faith in 'scientific' knowledge, which was a product of the positivist revolution at the end of the 19th century. The positivist scientific model, in conjunction with the epistemological authority of medicine, biology and psychology and their well-established place in the hierarchy of scientific credibility, both had an impact on the developing discipline of sociology. This was evident in that, during the mid-20th century, sociological thinking was often located within the same positivist, deterministic frame of reference. As a consequence, sociologists at that time also viewed the child simply as part of the **family**, separate from mainstream society, and as a passive recipient of the **socialisation** process.

It is only recently that other disciplines have sought to question the positivist empiricism on which developmental psychology and the bio-medical sciences were based. Notable in this questioning has been the contribution of philosophy, through the work on children's rights of Archard (1993), who identified Piaget's ideal of adult cognitive competence as peculiarly western, and of Matthews (1994), who argued that children are, indeed, moral agents, possessing the capacity for moral reasoning from an early age. Similarly, it is also only recently, since sociology has become sufficiently well-established as an academic discipline, that it, too, has been able to mount an effective challenge to such perspectives.

By focusing on the influence of structural determinants of behaviour, such as culture, class, **gender**, **ethnicity** and geography, sociology in particular was able to begin, in the final decades of the 20th century, to challenge the hegemony of developmental psychology and its central tenet – the notion of a general, unitary model of child development that transcends such structural variations. This new **childhood studies** developed in an entirely different direction, emphasising the **social construction** of childhood. Importantly, however, there also emerged an increasing unease within the discipline of psychology itself about the failure of developmental psychology to understand and take account of the impact of social and cultural contexts upon the development of children (Woodhead, 1997).

It is clear that children *do* develop, both psychologically and biologically; it is also clear that in studying and seeking to understand children and how they experience their childhoods, the significance of differences in their development must be recognised when studying the ways in which they exercise their agency as **social actors**. It has also become clear, however, that there is no single, pre-determined model of psychological development that holds true for all children, in all social, cultural and historical settings. The challenge for the social study of childhood is to bring together the developmental and social constructionist perspectives in a way that is complementary and enhances our understanding of the social and psychological development of children.

FURTHER READING

Archard, D. (1993) *Children: Rights and Childhood*. London: Routledge.

Archard, D. (2001) 'Philosophical perspectives on childhood', in J. Fionda (ed.), *Legal Concepts of Childhood*. Oxford: Hart.

Hendrick, H. (1997) 'Constructions and reconstructions of British childhood: An interpretive survey, 1800 to the present', in A. James and A. Prout (eds), *Constructing and Reconstructing Childhood* (2nd edn). London: Falmer.

Matthews, G.B. (1994) *The Philosophy of Childhood*. Cambridge, MA: Harvard University Press.

Piaget, J. (1950) *The Psychology of Intelligence*. London: Routledge & Kegan Paul.

Woodhead, M. (1997) 'Psychology and the cultural construction of children's needs', in A. James and A. Prout (eds), *Constructing and Reconstructing Childhood* (2nd edn). London: Falmer.

Woodhead, M., Faulkner, D. and Littleton, K. (eds) (1999) *Making Sense of Social Development*. London: Routledge.

developmentalism

Developmentalism

*The perspective, central to both developmental psychology and the biological model of childhood, that the nature and behaviour of children, and of childhood itself, are shaped primarily by their physical, psychological and emotional development and that therefore their development into adults is incomplete to varying extents, depending upon their **age** and stage in development.*

The social constructionist paradigm, which is foundational to **childhood studies**, provides the foundations for a critique of **developmental psychology** and the deterministic epistemology to which it belongs. The paradigm is rooted in the challenge made by sociology that asserts the importance of **childhood** as a social rather than simply a biological, and therefore developmental, construct. Its major contribution to our thinking about childhood has been to assert the **diversity** of childhoods based on all of those influences (e.g. culture, history, geography, politics, economics) that comprise the social context into which children are born and in which they grow up – and the importance of children as **social actors**/agents, with their own voices, who influence and are influenced by that social context. Nonetheless, the simple biological facts are that children do grow up, and develop as they do so, and that there are certain very clear biologically determined developments that do take place, which are central to the process of growing up.

This is easy enough to incorporate into the social constructionist model. However, we do need constantly to remind ourselves that not only are there many different childhoods, but also that their **social construction** extends to the construction of many and varied categorisations or phases within this single category of childhood; for example, a newborn, an infant, a babe-in-arms, a toddler, a child, a tweenager, a juvenile, a teenager, a youth, a kiddult, a young person and a young adult. These reflect different aspects or, as some would call them, stages of their development, both biological and social, but may be seen quite differently in different cultures. We therefore need to guard against simplistic discourses about childhood that are based solely on the **child**/adult divide, important though this undoubtedly is.

Arguably more problematic to incorporate into childhood studies is the nature of children's psychological development, since this requires us to engage with, rather than reject, at least some aspects of developmentalism. Particularly challenging are the findings of recent research on children's neurological development that have explored the impact on the development of children's brains of abuse and/or neglect and the neurological impairments that can result from this. As Glaser (2000) argues, there is now an accumulation of evidence that confirms a strong association between maltreatment in childhood and a range of social, emotional, behavioural and cognitive difficulties, including even psychopathology, both in later childhood and in adulthood.

It is now known, as Perry (2002) concludes, that the brain develops sequentially and hierarchically and that each area of the brain has its own timetable for development, the implications of which process are profound. In particular, the nature and quality of early life nurturing appears to be critical in the development of socio-emotional functioning. Thus, for example, if such positive nurturing is absent for the first three years of life, or of poor quality, a **child** that is subsequently adopted and begins to receive positive experiences such as attention, love and nurturing, may still not be able to overcome the malorganisation of the neural systems, resulting from the earlier experiences, which mediate socio-emotional functioning. This is because if the neurochemical signals that are dependent on early life experiences are disrupted, it can lead to major abnormalities or deficits in the development of a child's brain.

Such effects may mean that individuals who have been maltreated may find it difficult to cope with stress, to regulate emotional arousal, and to learn, memorise and achieve academically. According to Howe (2005), research has also shown that many maltreated children seem to lack empathy, a fundamental component of effective social skills and behaviour, for without empathy and the ability to understand the impact of one's actions on another, moral behaviour is difficult. Importantly, it is worth noting that children who have experienced serious neglect may also talk less about their own thoughts, feelings and actions than other children, which may have serious implications for **child-focused research** and for listening to the voice of the **child**.

In short, the behavioural and relational disorders that we have thus far understood in terms of attachment theory are rooted in the physiological and neurological development of the brain. Although such disorders may be modified or triggered by environmental influences, the evidence from neuroscientific research evidence suggests that they become hard-wired into the developing brain and can have profound implications for the behaviour of the children concerned and the adults they will become.

It should be emphasised that such research focuses particularly on the impact of poor **parenting** and maltreatment, both physical and emotional, on children. What it highlights, however, is the importance of the general processes of biological and neurological development in the brain as an organ, and the fact that these have a significant effect on the adaptations, behaviours and experiences of both children and adults. This knowledge should therefore give pause for thought about the potential effects of differential neurological development, consequent upon their different experiences of being parented, in children more generally.

Recent research undertaken at the Institute of Cognitive Neuroscience at University College, London, to investigate the development of relational reasoning also indicates that teenagers' brains continue developing for longer into adulthood than previously thought and that the structure of their brains resembles that of young children rather than that of adults. As a result, it has been argued that adolescents do not have the same mental capacities as adults because of high levels of activity in the pre-frontal cortex. This, it is argued, leads to chaotic thought patterns that are the result of teenagers' brains containing too much grey matter. Such findings also suggest that we need to consider carefully what we understand by the exercise of **agency** and the limits on this.

The existence of evidence which suggests that aspects of personality and behaviour are hard-wired into the physical development of children's (and ultimately adults') brains therefore presents an important challenge to our thinking about childhood as a social construct. It does not mean that **nature** rules, any more than it means that who we are is solely determined by our genetic makeup, since we know that our genetic potentials are only realised in the context of environmental, including social, influences. It does, however, mean that **childhood studies** must engage with the fact that key aspects of children's development do go through critical stages at certain points in their lives and that this has, in broad terms, normative implications for their development.

This does not imply that we must accept once more the dominance of developmental psychology in terms of how we understand children. Nor does it necessitate a rejection of the notion of children as agents. Accordingly, it therefore does not, and should not, be allowed to undermine our insistence on the importance of listening to the voices of children, or to abandon the fight for the empowerment of children and young people on the basis that they are, indeed, somehow lesser beings than adults.

It does, however, mean that we need to recognise that **children's voices** and choices, how they experience the world and how the world experiences them, are not solely a matter of **socialisation**, or of the **cultural politics of childhood**. It also means that we must reflect carefully about what and why children say and do what they do, and recognise that the sayings and doings of some are differently constrained from others and therefore perhaps have different meanings.

Such research findings also mean that we must embrace the fact that children *are*, in important respects, 'becomings' as well as beings (Prout, 2005). This, in turn, raises some interesting issues for debates about the **rights** and **citizenship** of children and young people, although this in no way lessens the importance of these debates. Perhaps even more interesting, however, is that such research also requires us to reconsider not only children's relationships with adults but also adults' relationships with children and, indeed, to think again about adulthood itself.

FURTHER READING

Dumontheil, I., Houlton, R., Christoff, K. and Blakemore, S-J. (2010) 'Development of relational reasoning during adolescence', *Developmental Science*, 13(6): F15–F24.

Gerhardt, S. (2004) *Why Love Matters: How Affection Shapes a Baby's Brain*. Hove: Routledge.

Glaser, D. (2000) 'Child abuse and neglect and the brain: A review', *Journal of Child Psychology and Psychiatry*, 41(1): 97–116.

Howe, D. (2005) *Child Abuse and Neglect: Attachment, Development and Intervention*. Basingstoke: Palgrave Macmillan.

Perry, B.D. (2002) 'Childhood experience and the expression of genetic potential: What childhood neglect tells us about nature and nurture', *Brain and Mind*, 3: 79–100.

Prout, A. (2005) *The Future of Childhood*. London: Routledge/Falmer.

Disappearance or Loss of Childhood

The idea that the differences between children and adults are becoming less pronounced and that this is creating problems for children.

It was Neil Postman (1982) who first suggested that childhood was disappearing, and in his analysis of the changing nature of **childhood**, he argued that technology was the key culprit. He suggested that it was through the development of printing that literacy was able to flourish, and that the need for **schooling**, to enable children to become literate, was a key factor in the separation of children from the adult world. Not only did childhood develop as a separate phase of the life-course because children had to go to school to learn to read, since they were, as yet, only reading apprentices, adults could also prevent innocent children from accessing particular kinds of information that they, as adults, deemed unsuitable. However, the later development of television was another matter; being a visual medium, Postman argued, children could access its information more easily and they could also do so independently. This meant, therefore, that the earlier controls that adults had over children's access to knowledge were diminished. And if children had the same knowledge as adults then, said Postman, childhood begins to merge with adulthood once more. And, for Postman, this change is not to be welcomed since children will not have the opportunity to develop, slowly, the morality and civility required for a decent society.

Other writers who also bemoan the disappearance of childhood do so from a more biologically deterministic stance. Writing in the 1980s, Elkind (1981) suggested that children's ready access to the media, especially television, would make them grow up too fast. Being emotionally immature, children are not able, he argued, to deal with early exposure to images of sex and violence and one of the consequences of this 'hurried' childhood would be feelings of insecurity and an inability to cope effectively with the strains and stresses of contemporary modern life.

Underlying both of these visions of the disappearance of childhood is the implicit **representation** of childhood as a period of **innocence** and dependency and, as such, these arguments fail to give adequate recognition to the fact that cultures and societies shape childhood differently. As Buckingham (2000) observes, for these writers, the childhood of contemporary children is presented as an apocalyptic 'distortion' of a 'natural' childhood, with commentators focusing on the risks to childhood from children's access to the **internet** and other electronic media, from **children as consumers** and, most of all, from the increasing **sexualisation** of young girls in the 21st century.

This vision of the loss of (natural) childhood takes up yet another form in some populist media reporting of children's childhoods in the majority South. As Stephens (1995: 9) observes, 'discourses of lost, stolen and disappearing childhoods' may be employed to describe the situation of children living in difficult circumstances of poverty or in war zones. However, while such living conditions may be far from ideal, the description of these children as being 'without a childhood' is not only emotive but also culturally insensitive. It fails to acknowledge the importance of the cultural context of these children's lives such that 'rescuing' children from these conditions may *not* turn out to be the most effective way to assist them. As Montgomery (2003) observes, the children who were rescued from Romanian orphanages, following the end of the Ceaușescu regime, were usually only the young and healthy. Older, disabled children were often left behind. Moreover, the rush to rescue children and to 'give them a childhood' obscured the fact that 'money would have been better spent supporting families, returning children to their care and investing in the whole country, rather than on rescuing a few hundred children' (2003: 205). Child-saving endeavours are to be found throughout the history of childhood and although many have been carried out with a concern for children's **welfare** uppermost, it is also the case that children who contravene current cultural representations of what childhood should be, such as orphans or **street children**, may not only be seen as in need of care but also as potentially damaging to the status of childhood itself.

FURTHER READING

Buckingham, D. (2000) *After the Death of Childhood*. Cambridge: Polity.

Elkind, D. (1981) *The Hurried Child: Growing Up Too Fast Too Soon*. Reading, MA: Addison Wesley.

Montgomery, H. (2003) 'Rescuing children', in H. Montgomery, R. Burr and M. Woodhead (eds), *Changing Childhoods: Local and Global*. Chichester and Milton Keynes: John Wiley/Open University Press.

Livingstone, S. (2009) *Children and the Internet*. Cambridge: Polity.

Postman, N. (1982) *The Disappearance of Childhood*. New York: Delacotte.

Rizzini, I. (2002) 'The child-saving movement in Brazil: Ideology in the late nineteenth and early twentieth centuries', in T. Hecht (ed.), *Minor Omissions: Children in Latin American History and Society*. Madison, WI: University of Wisconsin Press.

Stephens, S. (ed.) (1995) *Children and the Politics of Culture*. Princeton, NJ: Princeton University Press.

Diversity

> *The concept of diversity, when used in childhood studies, refers to the fact that within the social and structural space of childhood there are, in terms of the lived experiences of children, many different childhoods.*

Traditionally, sociology addressed **childhood** as a largely undifferentiated social and **generational** space in society that could be subsumed within the social institution of the **family**. Thus, apart from particular phenomena such as **delinquent** behaviour, **youth** gangs, and aspects of **schooling** and educational practice, children have traditionally lived out their childhoods, sociologically speaking, in households and as part of family units that are headed by one or more adults.

This is a perspective on childhood that has been buttressed historically by the dicta of **developmental psychology** and one that, ironically, has more recently been implicitly underpinned by the debate about children's **rights** generated by the United Nations Convention on the Rights of the Child 1989. Ironically, this also seems, on the face of it, to rest upon a universal and thus undifferentiated model of childhood. This is implicit, for example, in the possibility of a wide range of decisions being made in children's **best interests** in terms of their rights under the Convention that might not take account of the different cultures and societies to which children belong.

In the light of this, one of the key contributions of **childhood studies** to the study, analysis and hence the understanding of childhood has been to make clear that the notion of a universal and homogeneous childhood is a distortion of the reality of the lives of many children around the world. Clearly, childhood as a developmental phase in the life-course, which is typified by certain biological commonalities in terms of physical growth, some of which are broadly linked to chronological **age**, exists in all cultures and in all historical contexts. It is also evident that to varying degrees, different cultures at different points in history have recognised childhood, variously defined, as a social space that can be identified in terms of its generational differences from adulthood. Beyond this, however, childhood must be accurately located in its social, geographical, cultural and historical contexts in order to be understood in terms of the diverse, **global** experiences of those children who occupy that 'space' at any given time.

Thus, for example, we might consider contemporary childhood in the UK, as it is reflected in various aspects of social policy designed to provide for all children. Basic issues of income distribution and levels of childhood **poverty** are commonly presented in broad categorical terms. This identifies for policy-makers the percentage of children living in poverty. It does not, however, tell us anything about how individual children experience poverty on a daily basis; how they understand it as it applies to themselves and their peers; what effect it has on their **health**; and how they respond to and cope with it. All of this makes childhood a diverse experience.

Quite apart from this, however, it is important to understand the different effects of absolute and relative poverty on children from different backgrounds in terms of their social class and **ethnicity**; how **gender** might mediate the impact of these variables in terms of the lived experiences of boys and girls; and how the experiences of those who live their childhoods in inner-city areas differ from those in rural areas (Wells, 2009).

It is also important within this context to recognise that not all childhoods within families are necessarily configured the same way in terms of generational relations. There is a growing recognition, for example, of the increasing number of child carers who, on a daily basis, look after adult relatives who are dependent on them because of a disability or problems with their physical or mental health. The number of such **working children** who work as carers is difficult to know precisely, because often the extent of their caring activities is unknown; but in the UK, for example, data from the 2001 Census indicate that at least 114,000 children aged between 5 and 15 (53,000 boys and 61,000 girls) provide some level of informal

diversity

care to adults (Mayhew et al., 2005). Meanwhile, in Sub-Saharan Africa, 'the HIV/AIDS epidemic has led to millions of children being drawn into unpaid caring that seems to go beyond their traditionally and culturally defined responsibilities' (Evans and Becker, 2009: 14).

Such children carry enormous responsibilities, demonstrating the kinds of **competence** that are so commonly not attributed to them by virtue of their **age**. They also have to contend with the competing demands of those for whom they are carers, in addition to those routinely made upon them as children by their wider **family** and formal institutions such as schools and colleges. As a consequence, many such children experience relatively high levels of isolation from other children of the same age, a lack of time for **play** or sporting activities, feelings of loneliness, lack of support for and recognition of what they do, and subsequent problems of moving into adulthood, while those from minority ethnic groups face additional issues (Mayhew et al., 2005). The childhoods of young carers are thus not only very different from those of most other children but also very diverse.

That such diversity of childhood experience can exist within a modern, wealthy, industrialised, western society gives some hint of the diversity of childhoods that exist in different geographical and cultural contexts elsewhere in the world. Quite apart from the variables outlined above, a consideration of childhoods in, for example, Africa, Asia and South America and other countries in the majority South has to engage with phenomena such as **child soldiers**, **street children**, child prostitution and other working children that are unimaginable in the context of western childhood. When viewed from this perspective, the diversity of childhoods becomes apparent and with it, the dangers of viewing childhood uncritically as a universal and shared experience.

FURTHER READING

Baldwin, S. and Hirst, M. (2002) 'Children as carers', in J. Bradshaw (ed.), *The Well-being of Children in the UK*. London: Save the Children/University of York.

Evans, R. and Becker, S. (2009) *Children Caring for Parents with HIV and AIDS: Global Issues and Policy Responses*. Bristol: The Policy Press.

James, A. and James, A.L. (2004) *Constructing Childhood: Theory, Policy and Social Practice*. London: Palgrave Macmillan.

Mayhew, E., Finch, N., Bertesford, B. and Keung, A. (2005) 'Children's time and space', in J. Bradshaw and E. Mayhew (eds), *The Well-being of Children in the UK* (2nd edn). London: Save the Children/University of York.

Montgomery, H. (2003) 'Childhood in time and place', in M. Woodhead and H. Montgomery (eds), *Understanding Childhood: An Interdisciplinary Approach*. Milton Keynes: Open University Press/Wiley.

Montgomery, H., Burr, R. and Woodhead, M. (eds) (2003) *Changing Childhoods: Local and Global*. Milton Keynes: Open University Press/Wiley.

Stainton Rogers, W. (2003) 'Gendered childhoods', in M. Woodhead and H. Montgomery (eds), *Understanding Childhood: An Interdisciplinary Approach*. Milton Keynes: Open University Press/Wiley.

Wells, K. (2009) *Childhood in a Global Perspective*. Cambridge: Polity.

key concepts in
childhood studies

Ethnicity

> *The combination of characteristics derived from a person's geographic and hence national origins and heritage, which are acquired by birth and used to demarcate and maintain differences in background and identity.*

There is considerable room for confusion surrounding the meaning of ethnicity because of cognate terms such as 'race' and 'culture', which are frequently used interchangeably in popular discourse. This is partly because there is some degree of overlap between the elements that define these terms. Thus people from any given ethnic group will often also have shared racial characteristics such as skin colour and other physical characteristics, although it is self-evident that not all people with the same colour skin have the same ethnic background. Similarly, people from the same ethnic group often share the same cultural heritage in terms of their traditions, behaviours and attitudes: for example, their eating habits, food, styles of dress. This heritage is often reflected in similarities between their languages, religious beliefs and shared history.

While such cultural characteristics are often strongly associated with a person's ethnicity (i.e. their national origins and their place of birth) these are not necessarily the same, since groups having the same ethnic origins may not necessarily be culturally homogeneous. In addition, widespread international movements of population have increasingly resulted in the migration of cultures, so that amongst second- and third-generation immigrants, the differences between culture and ethnicity and the tensions that can revolve around these often become more apparent.

Ethnicity is therefore important in its own right, since it is a powerful element in the construction of personal identity – of how we define and understand ourselves as individuals. Ethnicity is also of significance in terms of social identity, because of the different social practices that ethnic identities produce and which they elicit in terms of the social responses of others (see, for example, Madge, 2006). Ethnicity is therefore also important in terms of the creation and recognition of difference. Within any given social group, shared ethnic origins, which may be reinforced by shared or similar cultural and/or religious backgrounds, often provide the basis for shared social identity, social practices and therefore for communities.

When ethnic groups exist alongside communities with different ethnic backgrounds, whether these be a majority or a minority in any given population, ethnicity becomes a powerful signifier of difference. Thus although to refer to an ethnic minority is to do no more than refer to the proportion of any particular ethnic group in a given society, in some contexts it has become a term of criticism or abuse. It is often based on perceptions of race, religious or cultural difference that may be only loosely associated with ethnicity. As a consequence, ethnicity can have a major impact on the shaping of individuals, not only in terms of their personal identity but also their life-chances more generally (see, for example, Bradshaw and Mayhew, 2005), since ethnicity can exercise a powerful influence in terms of locating individuals within any given social structure. Ethnicity is therefore an important conduit linking **structure** and **agency**.

Ethnicity is thus of particular importance in terms of the **social construction** of **childhood**. Once the notion of all childhoods being the same has been challenged, it is essential to consider what might be the key dimensions of difference and, in particular, the 'fault lines' in any given society that draw attention to difference rather than similarity, to social heterogeneity rather than homogeneity, to areas of social conflict rather than social cohesion. And it is issues such as **poverty**, social class, **generation**, **gender** and, of course, ethnicity that determine the ways in which any given society is stratified (Wells, 2009).

Ethnicity is thus one of the key components in terms of understanding 'the social structural child', a model that helps us to explore the diverse ways in which 'childhood' comes to be constituted in society for children (James et al., 1998.). It is also arguable from this perspective that the significance of ethnicity as one of these key components is amplified where it is not only a source of similarity but also of difference; that is, where groups with different ethnic backgrounds co-exist within any given society. A child born in an ethnically homogeneous society will, of course, experience a childhood that is shaped by issues of poverty and social class; such factors will have a fundamental influence on their life-chances, although not in a rigidly deterministic sense, since they will also learn to exercise their agency within the context of such structural influences. A child born in an ethnically diverse society, however, may find that their ethnic identity makes an additional and complex contribution to their daily lived experiences (Madge, 2006), as well as to their life-chances in the longer term.

Work by Scourfield et al. (2006), for example, illustrates that ethnicity can have a profound effect on the ways in which children are able to exercise their agency. In their study involving **minority-status** ethnic children living in Wales, they show how children negotiate their everyday social relationships, often down-playing their ethnic identities in order to try to fit in and avoid taking on an identity that their peers find unacceptable. By contrast, Connolly's (1998) study of an inner-city, multi-ethnic primary school revealed that race and ethnic identities could be used differentially by children and were sometimes foregrounded in order to retain positions of power amongst their peers.

FURTHER READING

Bradshaw, J. and Mayhew, E. (eds) (2005) *The Well-being of Children in the UK* (2nd edn). London: Save the Children.

Connolly, P. (1998) *Racism, Gender Identities and Young Children*. London: Routledge.

James, A., Jenks, C. and Prout, A. (1998) *Theorising Childhood*. Cambridge: Polity.

Madge, N. (2006) *Children These Days*. Bristol: The Policy Press.

Scourfield, J., Dicks, B.V., Drakeford, M. and Davies, S. (2006) *Children, Place and Identity: Nation and Locality in Middle Childhood*. London: Routledge.

Wells, K. (2009) *Childhood in a Global Perspective*. Cambridge: Polity.

Familialisation

> *The process of positioning children socially in, and focusing responsibility for their care, welfare and behaviour on, the family.*

As we argue in our discussion of the **family**, for many years western sociologists have located children, both as individuals and as a social category, under the umbrella of 'the family', rather than studying them in their own right and recognising their **agency**, and capacity for taking **responsibility** and autonomous decision-making. In many respects, this failure to problematise (i.e. to reflect critically upon) the concept of the **child** and the notion of **childhood** was a reflection of the dominant traditional social discourses and practices. This very 'invisibility' of children provided one of the main starting points for the emergence of **childhood studies**.

With the growth of alternative perspectives on and understandings of childhood as childhood studies developed, and in the wake of the United Nations Convention on the Rights of the Child (**UNCRC**) 1989 with the emergence of the idea of children as bearers of **rights**, children increasingly began to be viewed as **social actors** and, for the purposes of social analysis, as a social category in their own right, occupying their own social space of **childhood**. One consequence of such developments – the growing recognition of the **competence** of children and the debate about children's **citizenship** – has been the increasing importance attached, particularly in many European countries, to the **participation** of children in decisions that affect their lives, including matters of public policy.

In England, however, in recent years there has been something of a backlash in some quarters against the notion of human rights in general and children's rights in particular. This desire to return to a more traditional relationship between parents and children, and to reassert importance of the family as the proper place for children, has been evident in the trend towards familialisation. This can be seen in the 'responsibilisation' of parents, both in relation to **delinquency** or anti-social behaviour and to education. Thus, in spite of the lowering of the age of criminal responsibility, which means that English law now deems children as young as 10 to be responsible for their criminal behaviour, we have also witnessed in recent years a process that Muncie (2004) has termed 'family responsibilisation'. This has led to **youth** justice policies that focus on the removal of young people from the street and training for irresponsible parents aimed at compelling them to exercise proper care and control over their children. Some commentators have suggested that an informative comparison can be drawn between such developments and the 'strategies of control' that were anticipated by both Donzelot and Foucault. Similar trends are also evident in relation to **schooling and schools**, with the promulgation of polices that increase the pressure placed on parents to play a more active role in the attendance of their children at school and in their education at home.

One consequence of such developments and the reassertion of the family's traditional responsibility for caring has been increasingly to re-embed children within the private sphere of the family, to reassert the rights and responsibilities of parents in relation to their children and, in the process, to subdue children's **agency** and to undermine their **rights**. It is also to focus less on the child as an individual social actor and more on their identity as son or daughter, as the member of a family and a kinship group, a focus that is much more consistent with the organising principles of English family law.

In contrast to the general trend in Europe, however, the traditional view of the family and the child's place within it has remained dominant in many parts of the world. In many parts of Africa, for example, physical correction has long been seen as part of the socialisation process and of the training parents should give to children if they are to grow up into honest, well-behaved and self-disciplined individuals. Thus many adults, and children, accept and/or support the use of physical punishment on children and feel a sense of pride in its role in child rearing and sustaining family life and values. Thus, in spite of the UNCRC, very little has changed in some countries in terms of social policies and public attitudes towards such family practices, creating tensions between culturally specified traditions and the increasingly globalised (and particularly westernised) expectations of modern family life. Such tensions and concerns are not restricted to the majority South, however: witness the refusal of the USA to ratify the UNCRC for fear that it would undermine the traditional role of the family and interfere with the rights of parents to discipline their children or enforce their attendance at church.

FURTHER READING

Bainham, A., Day Sclater, S. and Richards, M. (eds) (1999) *What is a Parent?* Oxford: Hart.
Garland, D. (2001) *The Culture of Control.* Oxford: Oxford University Press.
James, A.L. (2008) 'Responsibility, children and childhood', in J. Bridgeman, C. Lind and H. Keating (eds), *Responsibility, Law and the Family.* Aldershot: Ashgate.
Muncie, J. (2004), 'Youth justice: Responsibility and rights', in J. Roche, S. Tucker, R. Thomson and R. Flynn (eds), *Youth in Society* (2nd edn). London: Sage.
Twum-Danso, A. (2009) 'Reciprocity, respect and responsibility: The 3rs underlying parent–child relationships in Ghana and the implications for children's rights', *The International Journal of Children's Rights*, 17(3): 415–32.

Family

A group of people of different generations who have been or are related by marriage and who share kinship ties.

Like many of the concepts explored in this book, that of the family is at once both obvious (we all have one and we see them all around us) and elusive, since all families are different. Family members will not usually live together throughout the family life-cycle, however, so that the sharing of the same household space is not necessarily helpful in thinking about what the family 'is'. This is despite the fact that, for many people, the strongest memories of family life are connected with the time they spent as children, usually living in the same household as their parents. However, growing up and leaving the parental home do not, of course, signify the end of the family; many older people continue to provide various levels of support for their adult children, sometimes well beyond middle age, and children often return to the family home at some stage. Thus the kinship ties on which the family is based, no matter how strong or weak these might be, still define the parameters of the family.

Most sociologists would agree that the family has undergone significant and rapid changes in the last two or three decades, and not just families in western industrialised countries, many of which have seen a steady decline of three-generational households. This is partly because of the increasing impact of globalisation and the consequent major economic changes that have affected most societies during this period, which have also contributed to significant political changes in some countries. It is also, however, because of the many and far-reaching social changes that have occurred. These are often reflected in demographic changes (e.g. in marriage rates, birth rates, family size etc.) which are a response to changes in medical and reproductive technologies and health care, as well as to the influence of social movements. One good example of this is the impact of the women's movement on **gender** relations and family life. **Ethnicity** is, however, an important variable, since children from minority ethnic backgrounds in the UK are still more likely to grow up in a household where three or more **generations** live together.

Linked to such changes, it is generally accepted that individuals in western societies have had increasingly high expectations of the close couple relationships they have entered into, and that this has also contributed to the spread of divorce and relationship breakdown. This phenomenon has generated a whole new set of variations on the family, challenging many of the traditional assumptions about the relationship between marriage, children and the family. This is in addition to other kinds of families: adoptive families; foster families; families based on same-sex couples rather than traditional heterosexual couple relationships; and families that are the result of the use of sperm-donors, IVF and similar medical interventions. As a consequence of such changes and of divorce, separation and family breakdown, a variety of 'new' family forms has emerged: single- or lone-parent families; previously married or never married families; and step-families. This has led to new terms for and about the family; for example, the reconstituted family, the post-divorce family.

As a consequence of such a proliferation of family forms, in recent years sociologists have begun to move away from the reification of the family and regarding it as a fixed social entity. They argue instead that we need increasingly to think in terms of 'doing' family life, rather than in terms of 'being in' a family or part of an

family

53

institution called a 'family' – in other words, we need to recognise that 'family' is a quality rather than a thing. Constituted through what Morgan (1996) termed 'family practices', the family is no longer seen as the co-residence of generations in a nuclear family: thus families 'are' what families 'do' (Silva and Smart, 1999).

The concept of family is clearly important for **childhood studies**. First, not only does the family provide the site and the **space** in which children are born and brought up but, because of this, for many years children as a social category have been categorised and analysed by sociologists under the conceptual umbrella of 'the family' rather than being studied in their own right. Thus, in spite of the impact of the United Nations Convention on the Rights of the Child (**UNCRC**) 1989 and the growing children's **rights** movement, it is still the case that in many countries, children remain heavily dependent in *every* sense on adults, in family settings of various sorts. However, by continuing to locate the child so firmly in the institution of the family, the effect is not only to mask or deny children's **agency**, their capacity for autonomous decision making, and their rights, but also to make parenting and the family synonymous (see Qvortrup, 1996).

This high level of dependence is also framed by a reluctance on the part of the State and public agencies in many societies to intervene in the private world of the family. It is in the family that children are located, and it is as members of the family that they are primarily understood; it is the family that provides the social and categorical umbrella under which, for so many purposes, children are subsumed; and it is the family that is considered to be their proper and rightful place, unless their adult carers are failing in their **responsibility** to ensure that their **needs** are being met. Underpinning this perspective on children and **childhood** is the belief, which finds expression in various ways, that since children are, according to the canons of **developmental psychology**, developmentally 'incomplete' and therefore lacking **competence**, they belong in the family and therefore they 'belong' to their parents. Thus **street children**, who are assumed, often wrongly, to be living without families, are considered to be at risk. Such views also ignore the situation of some children in the majority South. Due to the devastating impact of HIV/AIDS or war, some children are now effectively heads of families/households, looking after their younger siblings, with only limited help from extended family members. Others are orphans, living in substitute families or in institutions where the State takes on the familial role of parent, often reluctantly and with poor outcomes for children (Ennew, 2005).

These views of the family, and children's rightful place within it, have profound implications for the **social construction** of childhood and the way in which children experience their daily lives as family members. The 'responsibilisation' of parents, and the embedding of children within the family, often subdue children's agency and have also obscured children's perspectives on family life. However, recent research into children's own views of the family reveals not only the generational power relations (Butler et al., 2005; Punch, 2001) that are integral to everyday family practices, but also children's perception of their own contribution to family life and their experiences of **parenting** and being parented in different kinds of families.

FURTHER READING

Brannen, J. and O'Brien, M. (eds) (1996) *Children in Families: Research and Policy*. Lon
Butler, I., Robinson, M. and Scanlan, L. (2005) *Children and Decision Making*. London/ i
    JRF.
Ennew, J. (2005) 'Prisoners of childhood: orphans and economic dependency', in J. Qvortrup (ed.),
    Studies in Modern Childhood. Basingstoke: Palgrave.
Morgan, D. (1996) *Family Connections: An Introduction to Family Studies*. Cambridge: Polity.
Punch, S. (2001) 'Negotiating autonomy: Childhoods in rural Bolivia', in. L. Alanen and B. Mayall
    (eds), *Conceptualizing Child–Adult Relations*. London: Falmer.
Qvortrup, J. (1996) 'Foreword', in J. Brannen and M. O'Brien (eds), *Children in Families*. London:
    Falmer.
Silva, E. and Smart, C. (eds) (1999) *The New Family?* London: Sage.
Smart, C., Neale, B. and Wade, A. (2001) *The Changing Experience of Childhood: Families and
    Divorce*. Cambridge: Polity.
Thomas, N. (2002) *Children, Family and the State: Decision-Making and Child Participation*. Bristol:
    The Policy Press.
See also: The National Family and Parenting Institute: www.familyandparenting.org/index.php

Friendship

> *Children's affective social relations with their peers and others.*

Children's friendships and social relations have been the focus of attention since at least the 1930s when **developmental psychologists** began to use sociometric research techniques to discover the patterning of children's relationships with their peers. Concern over children who appeared to be social isolates within a group, or children whose friendships appeared unstable, stimulated researchers to plot out their interrelationships by noting down **peer-group** interactions. The resultant network diagrams were said to provide a visible representation of the ebb and flow of children's alliances with one another and thereby to reveal which children required interventions to assist them with making friends. However, as Mannarino (1980) has argued, there are sometimes problems with research of this kind. Depending on how it is carried out and the research methods adopted, it might simply provide an indication of which children in a group are the most popular rather than providing evidence of reciprocal affective relations between children that could be said to signify friendship.

Other research has, however, sought to explore the *nature* of children's friendships, with Bigelow and La Gaipa (1980) proposing that children's friendships change in type in accordance with age. Young children's friendships, they suggest, are based on proximity (who they are sitting next to at school, for example) and similarities of interests. Empathy – held to be a key component of adult friendship relations – they suggest is not present until children reach 11 or 12 years old when, during adolescence, loyalty, trust and respect become valued aspects of friendships. However, the idea that children's friendships develop over time in a series of stages, from unstable, fleeting relationships to more durable and intimate ones, ignores the fact that, even amongst adults, friendship types will vary from those of close intimacy to passing acquaintanceship. The meanings that children attribute to their relations of friendship, rather than simply the form they take, have, therefore, also to be considered (James, 1993). Indeed, some early work by Corsaro (1985) has already suggested that even quite young children of 3 or 4 years old can be involved in close relationships with other children.

The significance of **gender** in children's friendships has also been the focus of research. This has often drawn contrasts between the close dyadic nature of girls' friendships and the larger and more dispersed nature of boys' friendship groups. Characteristic of middle childhood, these different types of friendships are reflected in the different types of games that 6- to 9-year-old children **play**. Girls' close one-to-one friendships facilitate the more structured games they often play on the edges of the playground. Meanwhile, boys occupy the centre of the playground with large team-based games of football. Cross-sex social relations that include both friendly and more hostile behaviours do, however, take place. Kiss-chase, flirting and banter between boys and girls mark out the relations that take place in the public world of the school yard (James, 1993).

Thorne's (1993) research provides, however, a useful warning about the necessary assumption of gender differences in children's friendships. Through her ethnographic work in an American school, she shows that, like girls, some boys do also have close friendships. Others, again like some girls, can be loners. Thorne suggests, therefore, that there has been a 'big man' bias in research on boys' friendships. The very visible and assertive masculinity that is operative amongst some groups of boys has been taken as the 'norm' for boys' friendships, with assumptions being made that most boys do not have close, intimate relations.

More recently, however, Frosh et al. (2002) affirm that it remains difficult for boys to form intimate relations with other boys, given the stereotypes of masculinity which pervade boys' culture. Comparably, Connolly's (1998) work on race and gender in children's social relations explores male peer-group relations among young black and South Asian boys in an English school. While the former operated as a clique and were 'seen as aggressive, hard and good at sport ... walking symbols of masculinity' (1998: 97), the latter were forced into an excluded male role, akin to the position of girls.

Goodwin's (2006) study of girls' social relations in an American school, in contrast, reveals how the most popular girls formed a dominant clique within a particular peer group. Although the girls did have 'best friends', these dyadic pairings would also come together, at particular times, to constitute a larger friendship clique. Hierarchical, and with recognised leaders, its members shared similar social characteristics and the clique worked to exclude others from belonging. Thus, 'while clique members would permit girls in the inner circle to munch potato chips from their bag, Angela, the girl who followed the group but did not belong to it, was not granted even a single chip' (2006: 79).

What such research points to, therefore, is the importance of the peer group in children's **social worlds**. While it is not the only context within which children form friendships, given the structuring effects of the **school** system, which groups children into age grades, the resultant peer group necessarily shapes children's everyday social relations in some ways. It can therefore also shape how social groupings develop and friendships unfold. Thus, although not to be regarded as synonymous with friendship, the peer group provides the context within which affective relationships of different kinds develop.

FURTHER READING

Bigelow, B.J. and La Gaipa, J.J. (1980) 'The development of friendship values and choice', in H.C. Foot, A.J. Chapman and J.R. Smith (eds), *Friendship and Social Relations in Children*. Chichester: Wiley.

Connolly, P. (1998) *Racism, Gender Identities and Young Children*. London: Routledge.

Corsaro, W.A. (1985) *Friendship and Peer Culture in the Early Years*. Norwood, NJ: Ablex.

Frosh, S., Phoenix, A. and Pattman, R. (2002) *Young Masculinities*. Basingstoke: Palgrave.

Goodwin, M.H. (2006) *The Hidden Life of Girls*. London: Blackwell.

James, A. (1993) *Childhood Identities: Self and Social Relationships in the Experiences of the Child*. Edinburgh: Edinburgh University Press.

Mannarino, A.P. (1980) 'The development of children's friendships', in H.C. Foot, A.J. Chapman and J.R. Smith (eds), *Friendship and Social Relations in Children*. Chichester: Wiley.

Thorne, B. (1993) *Gender Play: Girls and Boys in School*. New Brunswick, NJ: Rutgers.

Futurity

> *The recognition, in the present, of the child's potential for being different in the future and the predication of present actions on the basis of this recognition.*

Futurity is fundamental to understanding many conventional adult views of and attitudes towards children, which are powerfully encapsulated in the notion of **childhood** and children as 'becoming' rather than being (Jenks, 1996a). The notion of futurity also defines the social **space** of childhood. Although the components of the experience of childhood and the parameters that define its historical, cultural, political and **social construction** vary considerably, childhood is universally seen as an apprenticeship for adulthood. Thus, in the same way that we cannot understand the concept of child without comparison with the adult, we also cannot make full sense of the child without reference to the child's future as an adult.

Childhood is universally recognised as the early stage in the human life-course and although we can, and do, differentiate between infants, toddlers, young children, pre-pubescent children, tweenagers, adolescents and **youth**, we commonly group all of these very distinct categories, which reflect important and varied elements of childhood **diversity**, under the overarching label of **child**. This is because the period of childhood as a whole, for children everywhere, is typified by physical, psychological, intellectual growth. Childhood is also a period of growth in a social sense; it constitutes a social apprenticeship, a period of **socialisation** and acculturation, during which children learn the necessary social skills and absorb the elements of their cultural heritage in order to enable them, at some point, to join and participate in adult society. There is thus a very real sense in which the child is, indeed, a human becoming.

The notion of futurity also implies that at some point there will be an 'arrival', a point at which the development, the process of becoming, ceases and the child has become an adult. Although the age at which this phase of the life-course commences in different societies varies, it is evident that in many, if not all societies, there is an 'age of majority', often marked by some rite of passage, at which the child assumes full adult status and the **rights** and status of **citizenship**. At this point, the apprenticeship is deemed to be over; the child leaves behind the social space of childhood, abandoning this to subsequent **generations** of children, and moves into the world of adults.

Futurity is also a central component to understanding the meaning and significance of 'generation'. To adults, with their various vested interests, children are not only future adults (as workers, consumers, parents, citizens, voters etc.), they are also the future *generation* and thus they are a form of social capital that represents 'the future' itself. Children are thus the inheritors of the legacy of the present generation of adults, a perspective that draws attention to the processes of social, cultural and **interpretive reproduction**. In other words, children not only represent the survival of the human species, they also represent the investment of the present generation in their collective future, their way of life, and thus the continuation of the enormous diversity of human societies and cultures.

In this context, decisions made by adults in the **best interests** of the child, and policies devised to ensure the best possible provision for children's **welfare**, must be understood not only as an expression of concern for the needs of children and as evidence of adults' caring for, nurturing and **protection** of the young, but also in terms of futurity. Thus, for example, the rights of children that are embodied in the United Nations Convention of the Rights of the Child (**UNCRC**) 1989 are not only about protecting them and providing for their welfare in the present and ensuring 'to the maximum extent possible the survival and development of the child' (Article 6); they are also intended to ensure 'the necessary protection and assistance so that [the child] can fully assume its responsibilities within the community … [and] be fully prepared to live an individual life in society' (Preamble to the UNCRC). Thus the provisions that all societies make in some shape or form to ensure the health, education and well-being of their children in the present – their welfare – are also an invest-ment in their future, as individual adults, and in the future of the society of which they will form a part and to which they are expected to make a contribu-tion at some point in the future.

These are powerful factors in shaping the **cultural politics of childhood** and are therefore key elements in understanding the process of social construction as it relates to childhood. From the perspective of **childhood studies**, however, their significance also lies in the fact that, because they focus on futurity, they all serve to diminish or detract from the recognition of the importance of children's experi-ences of the present and the significance of these experiences in shaping the adults they will become. The focus on children's futures and adults' investment in this can also blind us to their **agency** as **social actors** in their own right, something which, Lee (2001) argues, challenges the notion that children are simply 'becom-ings', apprentices waiting in the wings of adulthood.

FURTHER READING

Jenks, C. (1996a) 'The postmodern child', in J. Brannen and M. O'Brien (eds), *Children in Families*. London: Falmer.

Jenks, C. (1996b) *Childhood*. London: Routledge.

Lee, N. (2001) *Childhood and Society: Growing Up in an Age of Uncertainty*. Buckingham: Open University Press.

Lister, R. (2003) 'Investing in the citizen-workers of the future: Transformations in citizenship and the state under New Labour', *Social Policy and Administration*, 37(5): 427–43.

Qvortrup, J. (2008) 'Childhood in the welfare state', in A. James and A.L. James (eds), *European Childhoods: Cultures, Politics and Childhoods in Europe*. London: Palgrave.

Woodhead, M., Faulkner, D. and Littleton, K. (eds) (1999) *Making Sense of Social Development*. London: Routledge.

Gender

gender

The social and cultural construction of sexual difference.

While it is commonplace to talk about children as if there were a homogeneous group who share a whole range of common characteristics, paradoxically it is also the case that distinguishing between boy children and girl children is a key feature of everyday social practices in most societies. At the moment of birth, biological sex differences are noted and ascriptions of the child as male or female follow. The way in which such maleness and femaleness are understood and experienced con-stitutes 'gender' in society.

This distinction between sex and gender reflects a key debate in **childhood studies**: the **nature vs. nurture** debate. In this case, the question is raised as to whether biology accounts for the marked differences that begin to appear in the behaviours of boys and girls as they grow up, or whether this behaviour is **socially constructed**: that is, are they inevitable or are they a product of the different **socialisation** practices that boys and girls experience and the different patterns of social interaction and forms of social transaction that emerge from these? However, whether gender differences are believed to be 'caused' by biology, by society or, as some would argue, by an interactive mixture of both (Richards, 1974), they remain significant differentiating factors in the everyday lives of children. Their significance lies in the ways in which children interact with their peers and with the representations of masculinity and femininity that are available in any society; and how adults view children and understand and meet their **needs** and define their **welfare** as gendered individuals. This gendering of childhood occurs in and across a wide variety of social settings and media, ranging from everyday social practices at home, at **school** and in the neighbourhood, through to the representations of gender channelled through media of different kinds. In this sense, what it means to be a boy or girl child will vary in and between different cultures and societies.

But how do gender stereotypes of masculinity and femininity come to feature so heavily in children's everyday lives and experiences? Clearly, socialisation processes play an important role. Research by **developmental psychologists** from a behaviourist perspective has argued that children acquire gender roles through being rewarded for gender-appropriate behaviour. Others, adopting a more social constructionist model, have argued that children take on gender roles by observing and then imitating the behaviour of adults. By providing role models, and also by providing gendered **play** equipment, adults socialise girls into 'feminine activities' such as caring, through doll play, while boys take on 'masculine' behaviour by playing with cars and construction toys. Recent American research into children's engagement with the media revealed, for example, that the websites created for children by adults reinforced cultural stereotypes of gender in terms of the play opportunities they offered (Mitchell and Reid-Walsh, 2002).

The importance of gender is exemplified well in many studies of children's play and **friendships** and, as research by Danby and Baker (1998) shows, its significance appears even in the lives of very young children. However, drawing on the findings of their study carried out in a pre-school classroom in Australia, they reveal that 'gender is not an established social identity but a dynamic practice built and shaped by ongoing interactions' (1998: 178). Hence, they show how the older boys dominate the play spaces of the classroom through displaying their powerful hegemonic masculinity. This consists of threats of violence which, although frightening for the younger boys, in turn, initiate them into what it is to be a 'boy'.

This is not, however, solely a masculine trait. Goodwin's (2006) research among older girls in the USA shows how girls also exercise their power to exclude other girls from participating in particular social relations or activities. Like Thorne's (1993) work, which revealed a range of different behaviours amongst both boys and girls, such work provides an important counterpoint to a form of biological essentialism that suggests, for example, that boys are, by nature, more aggressive than girls.

Gender is, however, only one aspect of a child's social identity and thus gender subjectivity – a child's experience of him or herself as male or female – has to be seen in relation to other aspects of identity such as **age**, **ethnicity** and class. In this sense, gender is enmeshed in wider social **structures**, and the gendering of childhood has therefore to be understood in these terms also. As Walkerdine et al. (2001) argue, growing up as a girl differs in relation to social class. They show that this is not only in terms of different aspirations in relation to the achievement of 'femininity', but also the differential opportunities that are structurally available to working-class and middle-class girls with respect to education and, later, the labour market.

The importance of the wider social context in shaping children's acquisition of gender is amply demonstrated by dramatic examples, such as among the Canadian Inuit, where traditionally children might be raised as the opposite gender if circumstances were such that there was a gender imbalance (Briggs, 1991). Although not as common as it once was, it is still practised within some communities. In other societies where there is a strict separation between the sexes, the gender roles that boys and girls learn to take on may be highly specialised with, for example, boys learning to herd animals while girls begin to undertake domestic chores, as Penn (2001) describes for children in pastoralist communities in Outer Mongolia. Finally, gender also has important consequences for children in relation to their **health** and welfare. In majority South countries, such as China or India, where male children are often more highly valued than female children for social or economic reasons, female infanticide may be practised and boys' future well-being, in relation to the benefits of schooling for example, may take precedence over female children (see Stainton-Rogers, 2003). In all these ways, then, gender is a critical component of childhood's **diversity**.

FURTHER READING

Briggs, J. (1991) 'Expecting the unexpected: Canadian Inuit training for an experimental life style', *Ethos*, 19(3): 259–88.

Danby, S. and Baker, C. (1998) 'How to be masculine in the block area', *Childhood*, 5(2): 151–75.

Goodwin, M.H. (2006) *The Hidden Life of Girls*. London: Blackwell.

Mitchell, C. and Reid-Walsh, J. (2002) *Researching Children's Popular Culture*. London: Routledge.

Penn, H. (2001) 'Culture and childhood in pastoralist communities: The example of Outer Mongolia', in L. Alanen and B. Mayall (eds), *Conceptualizing Child–Adult Relations*. London: Routledge/Falmer.

Richards, M.P.M (ed.) (1974) *The Integration of a Child into a Social World*. Cambridge: Cambridge University Press.

Stainton-Rogers, W. (2003) 'Gendered childhoods', in M. Woodhead and H. Montgomery (eds), *Understanding Childhood: An Interdisciplinary Perspective*. Milton Keynes/Chichester: Open University Press/Wiley.

Thorne, B. (1993) *Gender Play*. Brunswick, NJ: Rutgers University Press.

Walkerdine, V., Lucey, H. and Melody, J. (2001) *Growing Up Girl*. Basingstoke: Palgrave.

gender

Generation

A group of people who belong to an age-based category.

In every society distinctions are made between older and younger people and, through using concepts of **age** to distinguish between people in this manner, different age-based social groups are created; these are known as generations. Following the early work of Mannheim (1952[1928]), it is important to see the concept of generation as embracing not only the actual experiences of people belonging to the same age group, but also their shared location as a group of people in historical time. By virtue of having been born at a similar point in history, the pattern of their individual life-course is likely to have been affected by large-scale societal events such as changing economic conditions, improvements in health care or the onset of war. For this reason, people can be described as not only belonging to the 'older' or 'younger' generation, but also as members of particular, historically located generations. In western Europe, the term 'baby-boomers', for example, is used to describe people born in the 1950s and, in the UK, young people who are said to belong to the 'Thatcher generation' will have been born in the late 1970s/early 1980s. This was when the Conservative government, under the leadership of Prime Minister Margaret Thatcher, set in motion a sea-change in the social, political and economic climate of Britain which has shaped, in rather particular ways, the experiences and life-chances of children born at that time (Pilcher and Wragg, 1996). It should be noted, however, that even within such a generation there will be different age-cohorts of children whose life experiences will differ one from the other.

However, the way in which each society orders the generations, and the relationships that exist among them, is not fixed. This can differ between societies and, in this sense, generations are also **socially constructed**. Traditionally, in some African societies, for example, a generational system formed the basis of their hierarchical political organisation, with power and authority vested in members of the oldest generation. Boys born at similar times would be designated as belonging to the same age-set and, over time, they would gradually come to replace the previous age-set of men who occupied the generational position of power at the top of the hierarchy. This attribution of power and wisdom to the oldest generations continues to be found in other societies (Japan, for example), even when generations do not constitute a formal organising principle of that society. However, elsewhere, such as countries in western Europe and America, the oldest generation may be less venerated and elderly people may be subject to processes of infantilisation (Hockey and James, 2003).

Though societies may vary in how different generations are regarded, it is common for adults, in general, to have power and authority over children and for children – the younger generation – to occupy a subordinate position vis-à-vis

key concepts in
childhood studies

adults. As Alanen and Mayall (2001) have suggested, because children everywhere occupy a position of powerlessness, it is important to explore the nature of child–adult relations from the **standpoint** of children. Adopting such an approach not only enables researchers to get to know about children's experiences first-hand, it also allows them to identify the generational systems of power that may often work against children's **best interests**.

Indeed, it has been suggested by Mayall (2002) that the study of **childhood** has to have the study of generational relations at its core, since the generational process that sets children apart from adults is what fundamentally unites children as a social category. Thus, in her study of family life, Punch (2005) explores how power operates rather differently in the generational relations between parents and children than in the same-generation relations among siblings. In her study, the children believed in the legitimate authority that parents have over children, which meant that parents could, to a large extent, exert disciplinary power unquestioningly. By contrast, the informality of sibling relationships enabled children greater freedom of self-expression.

In relation to childhood as a social **space**, in their cross-cultural study of contemporary European societies – societies that are said to be witnessing an ageing of the population – Jensen and Qvortrup (2004) argue for the importance of adopting a generational perspective. They speculate about what will be the outcomes for children's welfare for children who are born into societies that are characterised by patterns of declining and delayed fertility combined with increasing longevity. One consequence, they suggest, may be increasing pressure placed by the State on the importance of children's education in order to ensure a more productive workforce that will be needed to sustain the ageing population. Another consequence may be the increase in the numbers of children growing up without siblings if women delay childbirth until later in the life-course. This, they suggest, may have important consequences for children: as children grow up 'in a society where fewer and fewer adults live a life with children … it may be increasingly difficult to articulate the interests, wants and needs of children' (2004: 819).

The sharp division that is often drawn between child and adult generations is sometimes talked about in terms of the 'generation gap' or 'generational conflict'. Traditionally, this suggested that there were great differences between the **social worlds** of children and adults, and the generation gap was thought to account for difficulties in communication and understanding between younger and older people. However, the extent to which such gaps or conflicts are recognised as significant will vary between societies, as will the extent to which the differences between older and young people are necessary conflictual. Indeed, in late-modern societies, it has even been suggested that the 'gap' between the generations is decreasing, leading to the **disappearance of childhood**, as children and adults begin, increasingly, to share similar activities of the consumer market. The question remains, however, whether it is the gap between the generations that is diminishing or whether it is simply changing its character as part of the ongoing social construction of childhood.

generation

63

FURTHER READING

Alanen, L. and Mayall, B. (eds) (2001) *Conceptualizing Child–Adult Relations*. London: Routledge/Falmer.

Hockey, J. and James, A. (2003) *Social Identities across the Life Course*. Basingstoke: Palgrave.

Jensen, A. and Qvortrup, J. (2004) 'Summary – A childhood mosaic: What did we learn?', in A. Jensen, A. Ben-Arieh, C. Conti, D. Kutsar, M.N.G. Phádraig and H.W. Nielsen (eds), *Children's Welfare in Ageing Europe*, Vol 2. Trondheim: Norwegian Centre for Child Research (NOSEB).

Mannheim, K. (1952 [1928]) 'The problem of generations', in P. Kecskemeti (ed.), *Essays in the Sociology of Knowledge*. London: Routledge & Kegan Paul.

Mayall, B. (2002) *Towards a Sociology of Childhood: Thinking from Children's Lives*. Buckingham: Open University Press.

Pilcher, J. and Wragg, S. (1996) *Thatcher's Children? Politics, Childhood and Society in the 1980s and 1990s*. London: Falmer.

Punch, S. (2005) 'The generationing of power', in L.E. Bass (ed.), *Sociological Studies of Children and Youth*, 10. Oxford: Elsevier.

Global Childhood

The idea that children in different parts of the world share similar experiences of childhood

The question of whether there is a global childhood, which can describe or define the experiences of all children everywhere, is a complex one. **Childhood studies** has argued, for example, that childhood should be seen primarily as a **social construction**, a period of the life-course that takes particular forms in particular local contexts. However, at the same time, it also has to be acknowledged that childhood does have some more universal features. First, there are those arising from children's physical immaturity and their dependency on adults everywhere for basic survival **needs**. Notwithstanding that these needs are still open to some cultural interpretation with regard to the appropriate ways in which they are to be fulfilled, this does lend a certain global character to childhood (Woodhead, 1997).

A second global feature of childhood is that everywhere it is regulated by laws and by governments, and increasingly by international organisations. Here, for example, the United Nations Convention on the Rights of the Child (**UNCRC**) 1989 has played an important role, as children's rights have become incorporated into the local laws of different countries. Third, international charities involved in delivering early childhood services to young children in the global South are also, perhaps inadvertently, helping create a global childhood. Through their work, based on ideas about childhood that are common in wealthy countries of the

North, young children living in the global South are being exposed to these rather more globalising discourses of childhood. As Penn (2011) has argued, despite their good intentions, this approach to child welfare can create problems at the local level. Finally, as Qvortrup et al. (1994) have suggested, conceptually childhood can also be considered a universal, structural phenomenon. All societies have a **generational** space marked out for children which is different from that of adults, albeit that how that space is experienced by children themselves might differ markedly in different societies.

It seems, then, that childhood has perhaps to be understood as both a local *and* a global phenomenon (James et al., 1998)! One way to approach this dilemma, therefore, is offered by Wells (2009). She suggests that we think about 'the global' itself as structuring childhood at the local level: 'the global becomes one of several **structures** … that shape the lives of children and concepts of childhood in any specific socio-cultural setting' (2009: 4). Doing this enables exploration of the diverse ways in which all children, in their everyday lives, experience global **structures** such as 'the **family**', 'the **school**' and '**work**' differently in different societies.

The idea of global childhood also underscores the ways in which the phenomenon of globalisation itself shapes children's everyday experiences. For example, it becomes possible to see how worldwide economic systems connect children, living in different localities. In her comparative ethnography, for example, Katz (2004) shows the ways in which the same global economic processes are shaping the lives of children in New York as well as those in Sudan. Similarly, children's use of the **internet and new social media** is increasingly one of the global experiences of childhood, albeit that not all children everywhere necessarily have access to it. For those who do, however, these electronic media provide children with far greater and easier access to knowledge about other cultures and world issues than previous generations, while also enabling them to participate in global consumer markets. The must-have, much desired material object may now be the same object of children's desire in Thailand as it is in the UK.

Children are themselves also living more global lives, whether in transnational, multi-racial communities in cities or as migrants moving from one country to another. For such migrant children 'the media can serve as a powerful means of sustaining connections with their countries of origin … [and] also offer a means of learning about, and participating in, the new cultures to which they have come' (de Black and Buckingham, 2007: ix). In much the same way, Brembeck (2009) shows that going to the global restaurant chain McDonald's and eating hamburgers as well as their ethnic foods is one of the key ways in which immigrant children display their sense of belonging to their new culture.

FURTHER READING

Aitken, S., Ragnhild, L. and Kjørholt, A. (eds) (2008) *Global Childhoods: Globalization, Development and Young People*. London: Routledge.

Brembeck, H. (2009) 'Children's becoming in frontiering foodscapes', in A. James, A.T. Kjørholt and V. Tingstad (eds), *Children, Food and Identity in Everyday Life*. Basingstoke: Palgrave Macmillan.

De Black, L. and Buckingham, D. (2007) *Global Children, Global Media*. Basingstoke: Palgrave Macmillan.

James, A., Jenks, C. and Prout, A. (1998) *Theorising Childhood*. Cambridge: Polity Press.

Katz, C. (2004) *Growing Up Global: Economic Restructuring and Children's Everyday Lives*. Minneapolis, MN: University of Minnesota Press.

Penn, H. (2011) 'Travelling policies and global buzzwords: How international non-governmental organizations and charities spread the word about early childhood in the global South', *Childhood*, 18(1): 94–114.

Qvortrup, J., Bardy, M., Sgritta, G. and Wintersberger, H. (eds) (1994) *Childhood Matters: Social Theory, Practice and Politics*. Aldershot: Avebury.

Wells, K. (2009) *Childhood in a Global Perspective*. Cambridge: Polity.

Woodhead, M. (1997) 'Psychology and the cultural construction of children's needs', in A. James and A. Prout (eds), *Constructing and Reconstructing Childhood: Contemporary Issues in the Sociological Study of* Childhood (2nd edn). London: Falmer.

Health

'Child health' is a term used to refer to the health status of children as individuals, and also to the institutional arrangements and provision of health services for children.

Childhood studies has proved a rich ground for research into child health, through the raising of awareness about children as **social actors** and about **childhood** as a *social* institution as well as a **generational** category. Prior to the development of these new perspectives, children's health needs were largely framed by accounts generated from within either a medical or developmental framework. Social science research into child health saw it most often as a problem for parents and **parenting**, exploring the effects that childhood illness had on **family** life. An early example within this tradition is Vosey's (1975) account, which revealed how parents of disabled children endeavoured to represent their family life as 'normal' by de-emphasising the differences and demands that coping with a disabled child can make. In this kind of research, children with particular diseases or disabilities were often treated as a homogeneous group, whose experiences were dictated by the nature and progress of their condition.

It was only after children began to be seen as competent research informants in their own right that social science research started to explore children's own views of health and illness. A classic early account is Bluebond-Langner's (1978) ethnographic study of children with cancer, carried out through spending time with children on a cancer ward in the USA. Remarkable not only for its exploration of children's **social worlds**, this research offers a detailed account of how children learnt about their illness through noting the changing behaviours of the adults who cared for them. They learnt the meanings of particular hospital routines and came to understand the significance of certain kinds of medication. Through this, the children were able to accumulate knowledge of their own prognosis and that of the other children in the ward. They also developed strategies for protecting their parents from knowing that they knew. Later research has built on this pioneering work, using child informants to consider issues such as children's consent to surgery (Alderson, 1993), children's understandings of mental health (Armstrong et al., 2000) and children coping with chronic illness (Clark, 2003).

Policy concerns around child health are another important research arena, with epidemiological research seeking to establish the causes of, for example, low birthweight, childhood obesity and geographical differences in young children's health. Such research reflects a broader idea that child health is a problem of the State or, indeed, a more global problem to be tackled by research-based initiatives under the auspices of the World Health Organisation, UNICEF, or charities such as Save the Children. Studies of children's health experiences in the majority South are important since they help to identify the variety of social, cultural and environmental factors that might, in combination, lead to differential outcomes for children whose health risks are ostensibly similar. As Panter-Brick (2003: 102) notes, in parts of Nigeria, many women see diarrhoea in young infants as a 'normal sign of growth and development accompanying the milestone of tooth eruption' and may therefore fail to seek medical help. This could, in part, explain the higher rates of child mortality in societies where such beliefs are held.

In exploring policy aspects of child health historically, Armstrong (1983) examines wider issues of child health, locating these within a **social constructionist** framework. In western societies, he argues, the discipline of pediatrics developed from a late 19th-century specialism focused on the medical aspects of childhood diseases to one that embraced the wider monitoring of the health of the child population as a whole. With children being seen as the next **generation**, the State's concern was to ensure children's well-being and **futurity** through, for example, the introduction of compulsory vaccination programmes and of height and weight growth charts to monitor the development of babies, as occurred in the UK in the early 20th century. Such surveillance techniques led to the increasing standardisation of patterns of child development, which are used to identify 'problem' children (i.e. those who do not meet the norm).

While undoubtedly leading to improvements in health, as demonstrated by the low child-mortality and child-morbidity rates now common in contemporary western societies, if normative models developed in these specific contexts (such as those set out in Developmentally Appropriate Practice Programmes) are then used to measure children's health in the majority South, problems can arise. As Penn (2005) argues, these models have been generated in culturally specific settings – usually based on data from white, middle-class children living in the USA. According to Penn, this means that what is regarded as developmentally appropriate in one setting may turn out not to be so in another. This can lead to the misinterpretation of children's health needs and development in the majority South and to their inappropriate treatment.

FURTHER READING

Alderson, P. (1993) *Children's Consent to Surgery*. Buckingham: Open University Press.

Armstrong, D. (1983) *Political Anatomy of the Body: Medical Knowledge in Britain in the Twentieth Century*. Cambridge: Cambridge University Press.

Armstrong, C., Hill, M. and Secker, J. (2000) 'Young people's perceptions of mental health', *Children and Society*, 14(1): 60–72.

Bluebond-Langner, M. (1978) *The Private Worlds of Dying Children*. Princeton, NJ: Princeton University Press.

Clark, C.D. (2003) *In Sickness and in Play: Children Coping with Chronic Illness*. Camden, NJ: Rutgers University Press.

Fadiman, A. (1998) *The Spirit Catches You and You Fall Down*. New York: Farrar, Straus & Giroux.

Panter-Brick, C. (2003) 'Achieving health for children', in H. Montgomery, R. Burr and M. Woodhead (eds), *Changing Childhoods: Local and Global*. Milton Keynes/Chichester: Open University Press/Wiley.

Penn, H. (2005) *Unequal Childhoods: Young Children's Lives in Poor Countries*. London: Routledge.

Vosey, M. (1975) *A Constant Burden: The Reconstitution of Family Life*. London: Routledge & Kegan Paul.

Innocence

> Used to describe a state of being that is both naïve, in the sense of lacking in experience and certain kinds of knowledge, and free from moral guilt.

The 18th-century writings of Jean Jacques Rousseau are often regarded as the emblematic source of ideas of children's innocence. In his treatise on children's education, described in the book *Émile* (1762), he sets out a view of the **child** as being, by nature, innocent. Naïve and as yet unworldly, the child was, in Rousseau's view, susceptible to the corruptions that emanate from the social world. For Rousseau, this made **childhood** a special period in the life-course that needed to be nurtured and protected. It was a view of the child's nature that represented a radically new understanding of children and how they should be taught, challenging as it did the earlier 17th-century Puritan tradition. This had emphasised children's inherently evil nature: the child was thought to have a strong will that needed to be broken through strict regimes of discipline and training. Only then would children accrue sufficient 'godliness' to ensure security in the after-life.

This revolution in thinking about the child's nature that occurred in the 18th century was profound for, as Higonnet (1998) notes, the painting by

Sir Joshua Reynolds (*c.* 1788) entitled *The Age of Innocence* offered a timeless image of children's innocence that has become 'the foundation of what we assume childhood looks like' (1998: 23). The romantic image of a little girl, in a white dress, seated with clasped hands, gazing into the distance, is in stark contrast to the paintings of earlier periods. In these children are, for the most part, depicted like miniature adults, both in terms of their bodies and their dress. Usually portraits of children from rich families, they were used to indicate the children's future prosperity and status.

It might be thought, however, that the association of children with innocence has earlier roots within the Christian tradition, as exemplified in the Christ-child and in the Renaissance paintings that are decorated with baby-like cherubs and cupids. However, as Higonnet argues, while paintings of the Christ-child depict Him as 'humanly infant', it is clear that He 'omnisciently knows his divine fate' and is thus not 'psychically innocent' (1998: 18). The naked winged babies are also far from innocent: they are either depictions of non-human angels or representations of Eros, the pagan god of love, and are depicted in roles that lament death or encourage lust (1998: 17–18). The innocent child is, therefore, a **representation** of children that has its roots in western cultures and which had, by the 21st century, become celebrated across a diverse range of media – from advertisements for soap through to the 'cuteness' of photographic cards. This has, however, had particular consequences for children themselves.

An important distinction also has to be made between children as innocents and childhood innocence. Although there are clearly links between these two ideas, the first notion refers primarily to children's capacities and abilities. As **developmental psychology** has shown, from birth onwards all children gradually acquire cognitive skills through different kinds of social interactions and experiences that enable them to make the transition from a naïve state of innocence to that of **competence**. The second notion, by contrast, refers to the ways in which childhood itself is *culturally* and *socially* constructed as a time of innocence, something that varies between societies and which creates **diversity** in children's experiences. For example, as Montgomery shows, when we look cross-culturally, 'the cherished characterization of the child as sexual innocent is not ubiquitous' (2009: 181). Thus, as Giroux writes: 'childhood is not a natural state of innocence; it is a historical construction. It is also a cultural and political category that has very practical consequences for how adults "think about children"; and it has consequences for how children view themselves' (2000: 5).

In his view, the association of childhood with innocence is problematic in a number of ways. First, Giroux suggests, in practice, 'innocence' is not held to apply to all children. Since the epitome of innocence is represented by white, middle-class children, many children by virtue of their class or ethnicity may find themselves being demonised, with the social problems such as **delinquency** or criminal activity that are a condition of poverty becoming recast as individual problems. As early work by Ennew (1986) argued, the commodification of images of the happy, innocent child that are a central feature of much advertising, when used in the context of the majority South can have a demoralising effect on poor families who cannot purchase such a childhood for their own children.

A second consequence of the social and cultural construction of childhood's innocence is that children in western societies are, increasingly, becoming marginalised from the activities and concerns of the adult world. This occurs under the guise of their **protection**, since the emphasising of children's naïvety and their limited knowledge and understanding as inherent has fuelled notions of their special **vulnerability**. Taken together, these conceptualisations have set limits around what children are permitted to do, and how their **best interests**, **needs** and wishes are understood. Thus, although ideas about the 'innocent' child have their roots within the western intellectual tradition, childhood's innocence is becoming integral to the ongoing, global **social construction** of childhood that the United Nations Convention on the Rights of the Child (**UNCRC**) 1989, for example, is helping to forge. This has led to what Burman (1994) criticised as the emergence of 'disaster pornography': images of starving 'innocent' children, living in war-torn or drought-ridden areas of the developing worlds, that are used to mobilise support from rich donors. Thus, ideas of innocence are increasingly integral to the **cultural politics of childhood** worldwide.

FURTHER READING

Burman, E. (1994) 'Innocents abroad: Western fantasies of childhood and the iconography of disasters', *Disasters*, 18(3): 238–53.

Curtis, D. (2009) *Pleasure and Perils: Girls' Sexuality in a Caribbean Consumer Culture*. Camden, NJ: Rutgers University Press.

Ennew, J. (1986) *The Sexual Exploitation of Children*. Cambridge: Polity.

Giroux, H.A. (2000) *Stealing Innocence: Corporate Culture's War on Children*. Basingstoke: Palgrave.

Higonnet, A. (1998) *Pictures of Innocence*. London: Thames & Hudson.

Holland, P. (2006) *Picturing Childhood: The Myth of the Child in Popular Imagery*. London: Tauris.

Montgomery, H. (2009) *An Introduction to Childhood: Anthropological Perspectives on Children's Lives*. Oxford: Wiley-Blackwell.

Internet and New Social Media

Children's engagement with electronic media of all kinds.

The development of electronic media of all kinds by the beginning of the 21st century has offered children, like adults, many new opportunities for engagement with the world that were not available to previous generations. However, unlike for adults, access to computers, electronic games, the Internet and social networking sites is not always seen as a good development for children. Indeed, as with the arrival of television in the 20th century, they are regarded by some as a threat to childhood because of their potential to dissolve the symbolic barriers between the worlds of children and those of adults (Postman, 1983).

According to Postman, unlike the earlier development of the print medium which enabled adults to retain some control over the kinds of information children could access, the arrival of television – a visual medium – signalled the end to such control. With easy access to an increasing array of knowledge, the 'golden age' of childhood **innocence**, Postman argued, was lost. Others writers such as Elkind (1981) suggested, similarly, that through exposure to **age**-inappropriate material on the television children are able to grow up too fast, a developmentally based argument that suggests this will lead children to have problems later on in life.

These concerns about the potential **disappearance of childhood** echo those expressed by some people about **children as consumers** more generally. These anxieties coalesce around two key ideas: first, that children need **protection** from the adult world such that 'childhood' can be retained as a time of innocence: second, that electronic media, like consumer markets, will necessarily have adverse effects on **vulnerable** children. The first argument assumes a universalist, nostalgic account of childhood. It does not acknowledge that childhood is a **social construction** subject to change, over time and in space. The second, more technologically determinist argument, is similarly flawed. As Buckingham suggests, it rests on a view of children as 'passive and defenceless in the face of media manipulation' and does not consider the ways in which children as **social actors** might be able to choose to respond responsibly and selectively to their encounters with electronic media (2000: 38).

To counter some of the more hysterical arguments about 'toxic' childhood and the imminent death of childhood in the age of electronic media, researchers have therefore carried out a great deal of **research with children** to seek out their views and experiences. In his work, for example, Buckingham (2000) tackles the question of whether viewing violence necessarily encourages children to be violent. So-called 'effects' studies suggest that viewing television can have behavioural effects, emotional effects and ideological or attitudinal effects on audiences, and in his research with children and young people, Buckingham focused specifically on the emotional effects of watching television. He discovered that these were not straightforward. Although watching television provoked both positive and negative emotions in children, the consequences of those emotional responses, for individual children, could not be predicted. Children had a range of different personal strategies for dealing with negative feelings. Significantly, these were more successful when employed in response to fictional stories they had seen on the television; the children dismissed these *as* fictional. Feelings aroused by non-fictional material, however, such as documentaries and factual news bulletins, could not be so easily dismissed by them. In Buckingham's view, what is needed is not an approach that attempts to shield children from viewing certain films or television programmes considered violent or age inappropriate so that children can be kept in ignorance; rather, children should receive greater education in how to use media, and the information it gives access to, more productively and safely.

Similar concerns about the supposed threat to childhood arise in respect of children's relationship with the internet, and similar caveats must be applied. In her research Livingstone (2009) shows, for example, that there are opportunities as well as risks for children and young people on the internet. Although media attention is often focused on children's **vulnerability** while on-line (e.g. to grooming by paedophiles and cyber-bullying) the internet also affords those children who have access to it many opportunities and challenges. Without the internet they would not be able to participate in the **global peer** culture of contemporary childhood which, as Livingstone documents, can widen children's horizons.

Livingstone also reminds us that it is not the technology per se that produces 'effects'; rather, these arise from the social context within which technologies are situated and used. In any cultural context, children's everyday relationship with the internet has to be seen as structured by the nature of their own life circumstances, policy regulations and political aspirations. Emerging out of her research with children about their use of the internet is therefore a more balanced view that can counter much of the moral panic, as well as some of the unfounded optimism, about the role of the internet in children's everyday lives.

FURTHER READING

Buckingham, D. (2000) *After the Death of Childhood*. Cambridge: Polity.
Elkind, D. (1981) *The Hurried Child*. Reading, MA: Addison Wesley.
Livingstone, S. (2009) *Children and the Internet*. Cambridge: Polity.
Postman, N. (1983) *The Disappearance of Childhood*. London: W.H. Allan.

Interpretive Reproduction

The socialisation process through which children participate in the reproduction of society.

Traditional accounts of **socialisation** depict it as the process that teaches children about society and their place within it. In such accounts, this teaching process is largely conceived as one of knowledge transmission about social roles and behaviours that takes place from adults to children. Children's **participation** in this process receives little attention.

It was an increasing dissatisfaction with such accounts that, in part, heralded the development of **childhood studies**, with its commitment to more **child-focused research** through a focus on children as **social actors**. Interpretive reproduction developed as a theory of children's participation in social reproduction and change in this context, through the work of the American sociologist Bill Corsaro. Trying to understand his own fieldwork experiences with young children in the USA and Italy, Corsaro rejected the deterministic accounts of children's socialisation that gave little credence to the child as 'an active agent and eager learner' (Corsaro, 1997: 8). He turned, instead, to constructivist approaches to child development within psychology that tried to explain how it is that the child appropriates society, rather than vice versa. In his theory of interpretive reproduction, Corsaro draws, therefore, on **developmental psychology** and the work of those such as Piaget and Vygotsky, who positioned children as taking an active part in their own development. However, it is from Vygotsky that Corsaro derives the most insight since, for Vygotosky, social change is always the result of collective, rather than individual, actions as a result of people's interactions with one another. Importantly, Vygotksy argued that individuals appropriate culture and internalise it through language, which codes and classifies cultures in particular, meaningful ways. Thus, it is through learning language that, according to Vygotsky, children also learn about the society and culture in which they live.

For Corsaro, however, children do more than simply learn about culture. Through their interactions with one another, they also reproduce it in numerous innovative and creative ways and they do so, he argues, through interpretive processes that take place amongst groups of peers: 'the term reproduction captures the idea that children are not simply internalizing society and culture, but actively contributing to cultural production and change' (1997: 18). They are, however, also constrained in what they do by their very membership, as children, of their particular society and by their confinement in **childhood**.

From his ethnographic observations among pre-school children, Corsaro agues for the importance of language and cultural routines in this process of interpretive reproduction, since it is through these that children get to know their place in the world and to make sense of it. Core to this, then, is the social context within which children interact with others. Thus, in an earlier study, Corsaro (1979) is able to show how a little girl gains access to a group of children through employing her knowledge of the symbolic language of **friendship** and the rules of **play**: she says 'we're friends, right?' and immediately joins in, appropriately, in the ongoing play episode.

This leads Corsaro to develop what he terms the 'orb web' model of social relations which, in its spiral form, captures the recursive process through which both production and reproduction take place. Cultural knowledge is spread, like a spider's web, across a range of diverse social fields (education, religion, politics, economics and community), and at the centre of the web is the **family**. This is the core social institution through which children first begin to participate in society, although in modern societies, children quickly experience other social institutions and begin to participate in a range of friendships and **peer group** relationships of different kinds. Thus, Corsaro argues, 'individual development is embedded in the collective production of a series of peer cultures which in turn contribute to the reproduction and change in the wider adult society' (1997: 26).

The merit of this view of socialisation is that it avoids the overwhelmingly functionalist determinism of traditional accounts which positioned children as the relatively passive recipients, rather than the initiators, of social action. In this sense, it captures more closely the ways in which children can be observed living out their lives, whether this is learning about male and female roles through the acting-out of games of family life, or in discovering and displaying their knowledge about the social world and its rules through their play with friends. However, it can also be criticised in its failure to deal adequately with the constraints that social **structure** places upon children's interpretive and reproductive actions. While Corsaro acknowledges the ways in which the **social construction** of childhood positions children in particular ways through, for example, their institutionalisation in **schools**, and the structural contribution that this makes to society (see Qvortrup, 1994), his interest remains, primarily, in understanding the ebb and flow of children's friendships and peer relations with one another. He is concerned to explore the ways in which this contextualises their learning about the social world and their re-creation of it. And for understanding this, the concept of interpretive reproduction is an important one.

FURTHER READING

Corsaro, W.A. (1979) '"We're friends, right?": Children's use of access rituals in a nursery school', *Language in Society*, 8: 315–36.
Corsaro, W.A. (1997) *The Sociology of Childhood*. Thousand Oaks, CA: Pine Forge Press.
Qvortrup, J. (1994) 'Childhood matters: An introduction', in J. Qvortrup, M.N. Bardy, G. Sgritta and H. Wintersberger (eds), *Childhood Matters: Social Theory, Practice and Politics*. Aldershot: Avebury.

----------------- Minority Group Status -----------------

> *The minority group status of children identifies them as a social group that, in terms of its lack of political power and lack of control over and access to resources, is exploited and discriminated against, and is considered as separate and different from the majority adult population.*

In many western industrialised societies, minority group status is most commonly associated with issues of immigration, **ethnicity** and cultural or religious difference.

Perhaps the most common usage of the term is in relation to black and ethnic minority communities living in the midst of predominantly white and European majority populations, as in the UK and much of Europe. While reference to minority group status is important in the context of race, it should not mask the fact that such communities are not the only groups to be ascribed this status, for it also applies to minority ethnic groups such as Travellers and the Romany, as well as to others such as homeless people and people with learning disabilities, who are also frequently oppressed and may live on the fringes of, or outside, mainstream society.

The ascription of this status to children may therefore at first sight seem contentious when compared to the status of other minority groups. This conceptualisation has emerged from a consideration of some of the parallels between **childhood studies** and women's studies and addresses, in particular, the 'methodological and political questions about the relationship between the status of women and children as social minority groups and their constitution as objects of the academic gaze' (Oakley, 1994: 13). Such questions focus attention very specifically on the distribution of power between adults and children and the powerlessness of the latter.

In the context of childhood studies, the idea of the minority group status of children has a particular significance as part of the delineation of the theoretical field for the social study of childhood by James et al. (1998). Through this they sought to provide an analytical framework that moved the study of **childhood** away from its reliance on traditional developmental perspectives. By employing a series of dichotomies (e.g. voluntarism/determinism, agency/structure, local/global, continuity/change) they constructed the axes for a fourfold matrix that distinguished between four different discourses of childhood: the social structural child, the minority group child, the socially constructed child and the tribal child. These discourses provide an analytical framework for the analysis and understanding of childhood that moves the study of childhood away from its more or less exclusive focus on the child in the **family** and the **socialisation** of children: the child as 'becoming'. Conceiving of children as a minority group draws attention in particular to the structural and ideological issues that attribute a subordinate status to children and make them subject to potential oppression by those with power over them (i.e. adults).

Thus, partly by means of identifying children's minority group status, childhood studies has sought to highlight children as active social subjects, capable of competently exercising agency in a wide variety of situations but who are, as a group, widely excluded from many areas of social and public life. Seeing children as a minority group also enables their **standpoint** to be better considered, since account is then taken of their often weak and marginal position within society which, potentially, leaves children exposed to acts of discrimination. Such developments have played a part in shaping, but have also been in response to the changing international context in which children are increasingly seen as bearers of **rights**. Although lacking full **citizenship** status, children are now entitled to make legitimate claims for **participation** in areas of social life from which they have traditionally been excluded. Viewed from this standpoint, the minority group status of children readily becomes more apparent.

In what are claimed to be **child-friendly** societies, such as those in western Europe, it may still be difficult to conceive of children as a minority group, particularly in relation to the ideas of exploitation and discrimination that we have chosen to use in our definition above. In other geographical, cultural and economic contexts in the majority South, however, the evidence of exploitation, discrimination and oppression is stark. Consider, for example, the **sexual abuse** and exploitation of children in countries in the Far East, such as Thailand; the recruitment and (ab)use of children as **child soldiers** in Africa and other parts of the world; the widespread use of child labour, historically in the 19th and early 20th centuries in many parts of western Europe and America, and contemporaneously in many developing countries around the world; and the lives of **street children** around the world from Brazil to China. In all of these difficult areas, however, we must also constantly be mindful not to deny the **agency** of the children and young people involved, even though so often it is constrained by the exigencies of **poverty** or family circumstances.

FURTHER READING

Ennew, J. (2002) 'Outside childhood: Street children's rights', in B. Franklin (ed.), *The New Handbook of Children's Rights: Comparative Policy and Practice*. London: Routledge.

James, A., Jenks, C. and Prout, A. (1998) *Theorising Childhood*. Cambridge: Polity.

Oakley, A. (1994) 'Women and children first and last: Parallels and differences between children's and women's studies', in B. Mayall (ed.), *Children's Childhoods: Observed and Experienced*. London: Falmer.

Reddy, N. (1992) *Street Children of Bangalore*. New Delhi: UNICEF.

Richards, P. (2002) 'Militia conscription in Sierra Leone: Recruitment of young fighters in an African war', *Comparative Social Research*, 20: 255–76.

Nature vs. Nurture

Nature and nurture are often linked as an oppositional dichotomy in the debate about the extent of the impact of nature, or genetic predisposition, in determining the development of a child and her/his eventual adult self, as opposed to the impact of nurture; that is, of social, environmental and child-rearing influences.

The debate about nature vs. nurture is pivotal in understanding the human condition, but is perhaps most important in the exploration and analysis of **childhood**, the **child**, and the relationship between adults and children. The very fact that we can, and often do, refer to the concept of 'human nature' draws our attention to the belief that there are some fundamental and universally shared qualities in the nature of human 'being', such as aggression or altruism. Such qualities do, however, exhibit themselves with disconcerting unevenness in people's behaviour. Therefore, the fact that we are not all equally aggressive, selfish, self-sacrificing, hardworking and so on requires us to try to identify what processes might modify our natural tendencies or help us to learn to behave differently from how our nature might otherwise dictate.

The debate about the factors that influence a child as he/she grows up and the impact of these on his/her subsequent adulthood is not a new one. Heywood (2001), for example, cites evidence of this dichotomy featuring in discourses going back to the 12th and 13th centuries and of its reappearance at various points in history. In the later Middle Ages, he argues, people

> were familiar with the notion of the child as soft as wax, which could be moulded in various ways, or as a tender branch which needed to be trained in the right direction ... [while] from the Renaissance onwards ... [t]he idea that 'the hand that rocks the cradle shapes the destiny of society' became received wisdom. (Heywood, 2001: 35)

In the late 19th and early 20th centuries, positivist science challenged such views. It asserted the overwhelming influence of genetic inheritance and largely denied the notion of the child entering the world as a blank sheet on which nurture wrote the script of that child's subsequent life. Developments in psychoanalysis, through the work of those such as Freud and Erikson, began to offer 'scientific' challenges to the straitjacket of biological determinism, however, while **developmental psychology**, through the work of those such as Piaget, sought to bridge the gap and explore the relationship and interaction between nature and nurture in shaping a child's development.

At the same time, however, others, such as the educationalist Vygotsky, began to explore the relationship between children's social and cognitive development, challenging Piaget's views by asserting that children's social and personal experiences cannot be separated. More recently still, the work of child psychiatrists such as Bowlby has shed light on what is now known to be the universal importance of the relationship between children and their parents, and particularly mothers, for the healthy psychological, emotional and behavioural development of the child through the development of secure psychological attachments to their primary carers (Aldgate and Jones, 2006: 91 ff.).

Sociology, as the newcomer to the social sciences in the 20th century, sought to move away from the constraints of such individualised perspectives and to identify and understand instead the broader social mechanisms through which children learn the behaviours expected of them as adults. Termed the 'process of **socialisation**', this focused in particular on the role of parents and the **family** in achieving this transformation of asocial babies and children into socialised adults. More recently still, however, there has been a resurgence of biological determinism through new scientific evidence. This relates to issues such as the effect of diet, food additives and so on, on children's behaviour – what might be termed 'environmental determinism'. Perhaps more importantly, the mapping of the human genome has enabled scientists to identify ever more genes that influence various aspects of who we are and how we behave.

The history of the nature vs. nurture debate has therefore been one of continuous change, of evolution and revolution, as new evidence and ideas have emerged and reshaped thinking. Important scientific evidence in all this has come from twin studies: research that has identified and followed sets of twins, separated at birth and brought up in different environments, in an attempt to identify the effects of genetic inheritance compared to the effects of family and social environment (see, for example, Simonoff et al., 1997). Also important have been longitudinal studies that have followed the developmental progress of cohorts of children, such as the Avon Longitudinal Study of Parents and Children (ALSPAC) – often called 'Children of the 90s' – which for 15 years has been studying more than 14,000 children and their parents in the UK.

The debate continues to be one of great importance, however. Quite apart from cultural and geographical considerations, childhood **diversity** is such that because the development, health and behaviour of children can vary so markedly, it is important to determine how much of this variation is due to nature, or their genes, and how much is influenced by nurture (the environment children grow up in). This is all the more important in the context of the **rights** given to children under the United Nations Convention on the Rights of the Child (**UNCRC**) 1989, which are intended to protect children's development and assure their adult **futurity**. Important also are the social, health and educational policies and services that reflect those rights and which all States have a responsibility to provide in order to optimise children's growth and development.

The debate continues and it remains notoriously difficult to separate the influences of genes from those of the environment, but as Heywood succinctly notes, 'the most recent tendency in this debate … is to stress the interaction between nature and nurture, rather than to prioritize one over the other' (2001: 37). Similarly, Prout (2005) argues that **childhood studies** should now revisit the nature–culture dualism and find ways of recognising and giving significant weight to the ways in which the biological aspects of juvenility are translated into cultural conceptions of childhood.

The nature vs. nurture debate has, therefore, enormous significance for childhood studies: it shapes many social policies; it shapes parenting practices; it shapes adults' and societies' attitudes towards children; it is of fundamental significance in terms of the **social construction** of childhood and the understanding of children's **agency**; and, perhaps most importantly, it determines in large part many aspects of the daily lived experiences of children by framing their treatment at the hands of adults.

FURTHER READING

Aldgate, J. and Jones, D. (2006) 'The place of attachment in children's development', in J. Aldgate, D. Jones, W. Rose and C. Jeffery (eds), *The Developing World of the Child*. London: Jessica Kingsley.

Heywood, C. (2001) *A History of Childhood*. Cambridge: Polity.

Prout, A. (2005) *The Future of Childhood*. London: Routledge/Falmer.

Simonoff, E., Pickles, A., Meyer, J.M., Silberg, J.L., Maes, H.H., Loeber, R., Rutter, M., Hewitt, J.K. and Eaves, L.J. (1997) 'The Virginia twin study of adolescent behavioural development: Influences of age, sex, and impairment on rates of disorder', *Archives of General Psychiatry*, 54(9): 801–8.

Woodhead, M., Faulkner, D. and Littleton, K. (eds) (1999) *Making Sense of Social Development*. London: Routledge.

Needs

A need is that which is considered necessary.

As with a number of the other key concepts in this book, the concept of 'need' is difficult to define with precision, partly because the idea and language of need are so commonplace. It is an integral part of everyday life: we 'need' a drink, something to eat, to take a break, to have a holiday, to talk, to be with someone, to have a pay rise or an increase in our welfare benefits and so on. We talk about what we need in such a variety of contexts that, quite apart from distinguishing between what we need and what we want, it is difficult to compare the nature of these 'needs' in any systematic way in order to arrive at an understanding of what we mean by 'need'.

The above definition is therefore deliberately, and of necessity, brief. It does, however, invite consideration of some key questions. The first is that there may be an element of subjectivity in our understanding of need. This is because needs are contextual and, in spite of the imperative that is implied by need, may be more to do with wants and expectations than needs. Thus, for example, when we say we 'need' something to eat, if this is in the context of a western industrialised country, where people are used to having at least three meals a day, it may be more to do with the fact that we are feeling a little hungry having had an early breakfast and that it is nearly lunchtime. In this sense, need has nothing to do with survival. For those living in dire **poverty**, or in subsistence economies, or barely surviving in refugee camps, the notion of needing something to eat may be an imperative if the person is starving and struggling to hang on to life.

A second consideration is that even in the context of basic needs, such as food, water and shelter, needs can and do vary among individuals. This is partly because of different contexts and partly because of variations in individuals' **resilience** – some people are better able to cope, either without or with lesser amounts of basic provisions. Thus, for example, an individual's need for shelter, or for food and water, will differ depending upon **age**, upon their health, upon where they are living and upon the survival skills they have learned. So the second question is: for whom is something a need?

The third key question is by whom something is considered necessary. An individual's 'need' to give up smoking, to drink less alcohol, or to eat a healthy balanced diet may be a need defined by a doctor or other health professional; our 'need' to make less use of private cars or reduce our amount of air travel may be defined by politicians and/or scientists concerned about climate change; a child's 'need' for education (or for education of a particular type or to a particular level) may be defined in one way, in one particular economic, political, economic and cultural context by politicians, and in another way by parents; and a child's 'need' for a new pair of trainers is certainly going to be defined differently by different 'others' (parents and peers, for example) in different contexts!

Such considerations underscore several important points about needs. There is a hierarchy of basic needs (Maslow, 1943), which helps us identify and prioritise the essential elements for human survival, that is, both individually and collectively, as a species. In addition to such basic needs, there are needs for services, such as power, sanitation and so on. These have come to be seen in western industrialised societies as essential needs, but this is specific to the particular set of political and economic variables that define these as needs in the context of advanced societies. Such needs are therefore defined as necessities in the context of the overall economic and social development of particular countries, rather than being universal and basic needs without which survival is impossible. Like poverty, therefore, needs such as these are relative. However, in any given society, there is usually a recognition that all members of that society, be they adults or children, have the same needs, even if the recognition of this in principle is not necessarily reflected in practice because of an unequal distribution of resources.

Beyond this, there are psychological and social needs that are rooted in our nature as social animals ,and it is perhaps in this area more than any other that we come back to the issue implied by the second question above (i.e. do children have needs that differ from those of adults?). It is clear that even in terms of their basic needs (shelter, food, warmth etc.) some children's needs differ from those of adults in any given society because of their **futurity**. In other words, for children to grow up and achieve their full potential as adults, they have special physical needs in terms of nutrition, clothing and health care; special social needs in terms of **schooling**, **socialisation** and moral development; and special psychological needs in terms of **protection**, nurturing and attachment. However, as Woodhead (1997) has argued, beyond basic survival needs, the ways in which other needs are met – or even conceptualised as children's needs – vary cross-culturally. As he says, 'In short, while in certain very general respects, "needs" statements may have universal validity, detailed prescriptions about children's needs are normative, and depend on a judgment about processes of cultural adaptation and social adjustment' (1997: 73–4).

It is because children's needs are seen by adults to be so important for children everywhere, and because children in many contexts are not able to meet these needs without adult assistance, that they are embodied as **rights** in the context of the United Nations Convention on the Rights of the Child (**UNCRC**) 1989. It is important, however, to recognise that not all rights, including children's rights, are necessarily needs-based: as noted above, children's **competence** and ability to meet at least some of these different child-specific needs, and their **resilience** in terms of their ability to survive if these are not met, vary between different social and cultural contexts.

The embodiment of children's needs into a rights framework reflects a significant shift in the debate about their needs. Hitherto, the meeting of children's needs was an issue that was most commonly considered in the context of discourses of **welfare**. In essence, this placed children in a totally dependent role in relation to adults, who in theory had the **responsibility** for ensuring that children's welfare needs were met. It has been argued, however, that 'the welfare model has failed children' (Lansdown, 2005: 122) and that the incorporation of children's needs into a rights framework is important since it makes clear that children have a *right* to have those needs met. They no longer depend upon adults to define the dimensions of their welfare and provide for their needs at their discretion.

It is also important to recognise the limitations of such a rights framework, in the sense that adults' perceptions of children's needs may differ from those of children themselves. Although **childhood studies** has begun to shed some light upon this, as yet 'there has been little engagement with children themselves about things that they themselves would consider essential for their material and social well-being' (Ridge, 2005: 110).

FURTHER READING

Lansdown, G. (2005) 'Children's welfare and children's rights', in H. Hendrick (ed.), *Child Welfare and Social Policy: An Essential Reader*. Bristol: The Policy Press.

Maslow, A.H. (1943) 'A theory of human motivation', *Psychological Review*, 50: 370–96.

Ridge, T. (2005) 'The challenge of child poverty: Developing a child-centred approach', in H. Hendrick (ed.), *Child Welfare and Social Policy: An Essential Reader*. Bristol: The Policy Press.

UNICEF (2007) *Child Poverty in Perspective: An Overview of Child Well-being in Rich Countries*, Innocenti Report Card 7, UNICEF Innocenti Research Centre. Florence: United Nations Children's Fund.

Woodhead, M. (1997) 'Psychology and the cultural construction of children's needs', in A. James and A. Prout (eds), *Constructing and Reconstructing Childhood* (2nd edn). Basingstoke: Falmer.

neglect

Neglect is indifference towards, or the failure to care for or attend to, a person, duty or task.

In the case of a **child**, neglect is the persistent failure to meet her/his basic physical and/or psychological **needs**, such that it will have a serious impact on her/his **health** or development and may even result in a child's death. It can include the failure to provide adequately for the child's basic needs, such as food, shelter or clothing, failure to protect her/him from physical harm or danger, failing to provide suitable medical care or treatment. It can also include the neglect of, or a failure to respond to, a child's emotional needs, cognitive neglect (the failure to recognise and therefore respond appropriately to the emotional needs of the child) in infancy being of particular importance because of its long-lasting effects on the development of the brain (see also **developmentalism**). Neglect is therefore often linked with emotional abuse.

It is clear that these various forms of neglect raise different issues in terms of the kind of response needed and the speed of that response. For example, activity or neglect in certain areas of child care can endanger children's lives and therefore the wilful failure to provide adequate medical treatment, for example, whether by failing to provide treatment or refusing to agree to it, may become a criminal matter regardless of the parents' reasons. And since babies and very young children can die very quickly if they become ill, the threshold for neglect for them may be very different from that for older children. Thus, although the long-term consequences of emotional neglect can be very serious, if not actually life-threatening, it may be argued this kind of neglect requires less urgent intervention than threats to a child's health.

What constitutes neglect can vary not only according to a child's **age**, but also according to culture and traditions in child care (Montgomery, 2009). Thus, for example, in some societies, to place an infant to sleep on its own in a room, or to allow it to cry without parental response, would be viewed as neglect, whereas these practices are relatively common in western industrialised societies. Here, because of the risk of smothering, falling asleep with a child may be viewed as poor child care, and responding instantly to a crying child as indulgent. Similarly, parents of **street children** would be seen as neglectful in some societies but not others. Neglect of different kinds is also differently distributed within societies. Thus, while emotional neglect can be a feature of any **family**, regardless of social status or economic position, the failure to meet a child's basic physical needs is more commonly associated with **poverty**, although material disadvantage does not necessarily lead to neglect.

In the UK, the notion of child neglect began to emerge in Victorian society as, with the development of organisations such as the National Society for the Prevention of Cruelty to Children (NSPCC), the understanding of child **welfare** and child abuse became more sophisticated and moved beyond simple cruelty to include, for example, the neglect of children by drunken parents. Indeed, for many decades prior to the emergence of the 'battered baby syndrome' and 'non-accidental injury' in the 1960s, and the subsequent focus on the physical abuse of children and its medicalisation, neglect was the dominant focus of child welfare and **protection** polices, being linked, as it was in the context of the welfare state, to issues of the problem family, poverty, deprivation and the social consequences of these in terms of issues such as **delinquency**.

More recently in the UK and elsewhere, the debate about child protection has seen a re-emergence of concerns about neglect that has led to this becoming more prominent as a reason for State intervention in family life. Such concerns have been underlined by the growing awareness of the debate about children's **rights**. Thus, for example, Article 6 of the United Nations Convention on the Rights of the Child (**UNCRC**) 1989, which is one of the general principles of the Convention, requires States Parties to 'ensure to the maximum extent possible the … development of the child', a provision that has particular implications for the issue of neglect. Similarly, Article 24 provides the child's right to health and health services. It is also arguable that the provisions for the development of the child in Article 27, which addresses the standard of living required for the child's 'physical, mental, spiritual, moral and social development', and the developmental aims for education outlined in Article 29 are also relevant in the contextualisation and understanding of neglect. However, the focus on children's rights and State intervention in family life resulting from this has led to increasing tension with those who seek to defend the privacy of the family and parental rights (see also **familialisation**).

Neglect remains difficult to define, however, as are the parameters of risk associated with various forms of neglect and the extent of any harm caused. In the UK, for example, any neglect must be deemed to have led to 'significant harm'. This may seem to be relatively easy to determine in terms of physical neglect, but growing concerns about childhood obesity have led some to argue that parental failure to provide proper nutritional care might also constitute a form of neglect that could lead to State intervention. The failure of a child to thrive as a result of parental neglect is also a very difficult issue to identify, while emotional neglect, which is recognised to be a major cause of long-term harm to the development of children, is perhaps the most difficult form of neglect to identify and deal with. Nonetheless, research indicates that neglect by parents is the most common form of abuse, in the UK and elsewhere.

FURTHER READING

Fortin, J. (2003) *Children's Rights and the Developing Law* (2nd edn). London: LexisNexis.

Gibbons, J., Conroy, S. and Bell, C. (1995) *Operating the Child Protection System*. London: HMSO.

Iwaniec, D. (2006) *The Emotionally Abused and Neglected Child: Identification, Assessment and Intervention – A Practice Handbook*. Chichester: Wiley.

Montgomery, H. (2009) *An Introduction to Childhood: Anthropological Perspectives*. Oxford: Wiley Blackwell.

Parton, N. (2006) *Safeguarding Childhood: Early Intervention and Surveillance in a Late Modern Society*. London: Palgrave.

Wilson, K. and James, A.L. (eds) (2007) *The Child Protection Handbook*. London/Edinburgh: Elsevier/Ballière-Tindall.

neglect

Commonly used to embrace and describe the wide range of physical, social, psychological and emotional transactions that take place in the context of the family
between parent and child during the years in which the child is dependent on the
parent. As such it is both descriptive – identifying and illustrating what parents 'do'
in relation to their children – and prescriptive, in the sense of defining that which
parents are expected to do in order to fulfil their social, legal and other obligations
in any given cultural context.

As with many of the other key concepts in this book, 'parenting' is difficult to
define accurately and in its entirety, not least because, as with **child** and **childhood**,
we all know from our first-hand experience of being parented as a child what
parenting is and who 'did it' to us. Thus, as is so often the case, that with which we
are most familiar – which we take most for granted as part of our everyday life,
which is fundamental to our understanding of who we are as individuals and how
we came to be as we are – often proves to be the most elusive when it comes to
describing, defining and 'objectively' analysing it as a concept. A key question in
understanding parenting is, therefore, inevitably: 'What is a parent?' (Bainham
et al., 1999).

The first point to make is that being a parent and parenting have social, psychological and legal dimensions, all of which vary between cultures. Arising from this,
the second point is that although the relationship between the child and parents
has firm biological roots, it also has clear social dimensions that may be equally
strong. This is the case, essentially, in the sense that a child may have a biological
parent who plays little or no active part in those activities that are described as
child-rearing (see below), and they may also have a substitute or surrogate parent
who actively fulfils the social role of parent. Thus, for example, a child may have
a step-parent, or a substitute carer such as a nanny or a grandparent, who to all
intents and purposes 'parents' the child. In such circumstances, the role of the parent substitute and the parenting they provide is the range of nurturing and child-
rearing experiences that a child needs for their social, psychological and emotional
development.

As suggested by the definition we have offered, parenting is also something that
is situated primarily in the relatively private social and emotional space provided
by the **family**, which provides the primary locus in the early years of a child's life
for the processes of **socialisation**. In addition, in so far as the roles, responsibilities
and activities that comprise parenting are largely associated with the development
of the child during the early years of the life-course, and thus with nurture, parenting as an *activity* generally declines steeply and often ceases altogether after the
child has become an adult and, in particular, has left the family home. The
parent–child relationship still continues, of course, but parenting as an activity is

key concepts in
childhood studies

often heavily circumscribed once the child becomes economically, socially and psychologically independent.

Such processes are obviously also clearly reflected in the legal construction of the rights and responsibilities of parents vis-à-vis their children. As Bainham et al. (1999) argue in the context of the England and Wales, parental responsibility is defined as a technical legal concept that includes the rights, duties, powers, responsibility and authority in relation to a child and his/her property. Similar definitions are to be found in legal systems around the world. These rights, duties, powers and responsibilities cease, however, once the child reaches the legal **age** of majority when they assume the **rights** and responsibilities of **citizenship**, independently and in their own right, as opposed to their being granted to them through their parents as members of a family. Although the nature of the legal cultures and systems that define the relationship between parents and children will vary between cultures, the law, as a mechanism for the social regulation and control of relationships (James and James, 2004), provides an important reference point in terms of defining the parameters of parenting.

For example, it has an important role to play in child **protection**, since in many countries it is only through and in the context of law that the State is able to intervene in the private world of the family. This is in cases where parents are seen to be failing to meet their responsibilities actively to provide for the **needs** of their children or to ensure that their rights (e.g. the right to be protected against abuse) are acknowledged and secured. Given the extent of childhood **diversity**, whether in terms of **poverty**, **ethnicity** or their widely varied **social worlds**, the judgement about what constitutes good parenting is often a difficult one to make, a fact that is reflected in the emergence of the notion of 'good-enough parenting'.

The law also has a wider social control function in relation to parenting; for example, in relation to children who become involved in **delinquency**. In many countries, parents are expected to take some **responsibility** for such behaviour on the part of their children, although the extent to which this is the case varies in different cultural and historical contexts. In the UK, for example, there has recently been a trend towards the 'responsibilisation' of the family and increasingly holding parents responsible for their children's misdemeanours. Thus, as Gelsthorpe has argued, recent UK legislation has reflected growing criticism of those parents who fail to meet their responsibility to society 'to produce moral upstanding citizens … and "good families"' (1999: 236). Such developments can reveal important shifts in the **cultural politics of childhood** in any given society and there is little doubt that, in the case of the UK, they reflect a profound ambivalence towards the notion of children as bearers of rights and the complementary perspective offered by **childhood studies** of children as competent **social actors**.

But what about children's own experiences of being parented? Given the 'welfarist' model within which parenting is usually framed, there is still relatively little research that has explored this, since children are so often 'envisaged as passive recipients of "outcomes" of the process of parenting' (James, 1999: 183). However, research such as that by Smart et al. (2001) and Näsman (2003) is beginning to explore parenting from children's **standpoint**, providing new insights that are enriching our understanding. Thus, for example, in their research into English children's experiences of divorce, Smart et al. (2001) found that children emphasised that what is important to them is the knowledge that their parents love and care for them. This makes it easier for children to manage the absence of one parent from the family home. Näsman, on the other hand, explores Swedish children's experiences of being parented in families changed by unemployment, and here she shows how children learn to recognise and cope with their parents' moods. Indeed, they often 'take the role of the parent and empathetically share their experiences', thereby actively helping to manage the difficulties in their family life (Näsman, 2003: 56).

FURTHER READING

Bainham, A., Day Sclater, S. and Richards, M. (eds) (1999) *What Is a Parent? A Socio-Legal Analysis*. Oxford: Hart.

Butler, I., Robinson, M. and Scanlan, L. (2005) *Children and Decision Making*. London/York: NCB/JRF.

Gelsthorpe, L. (1999) 'Youth crime and parental responsibility', in A. Bainham, S. Day Sclater and M. Richards (eds), *What is a Parent? A Socio-Legal Analysis*. Oxford: Hart.

James, A. (1999) 'Parents: A children's perspective', in A. Bainham, S. Day Sclater and M. Richards (eds), *What is a Parent? A Socio-Legal Analysis*. Oxford: Hart.

James, A. and James, A.L. (2004) *Constructing Childhood: Theory, Policy and Social Practice*. London: Palgrave Macmillan.

Näsman, E. (2003) 'Employed or unemployed parents: A child perspective', in A. Jensen and L. McKee (eds), *Children and the Changing Family: Between Transformation and Negotiation*. London: Routledge/Falmer.

Smart, C., Neale, B. and Wade, A. (2001) *The Changing Experience of Childhood*. Cambridge: Polity.

See also: The National Family and Parenting Institute: www.familyandparenting.org/index.php.

Participation

> *To take part in and to contribute actively to a situation, an event, a process or an outcome, although the extent of the contribution and the autonomy with which it is made may vary considerably and may be constrained in various ways.*

Participation is another everyday and widely understood concept that assumes particular significance in the context of **childhood studies** because in many societies, children's ability to participate is limited to clearly defined social **spaces**, most of which are policed and regulated by adults. One of the main reasons why children's participation has become a matter of importance, however, is the growing discourse about children's **rights** and, in particular, the significance of the United Nations Convention on the Rights of the Child (**UNCRC**) 1989 in defining what have come to be termed children's 'participation rights'. Article 12 of the Convention states that:

> States parties shall assure to the child who is capable of forming his or her own views the right to express those views freely in all matters affecting the child, the views of the child being given due weight in accordance with the age and maturity of the child.

> For this purpose that child shall in particular be provided with the opportunity to be heard in any judicial and administrative proceedings affecting the child, either directly, or through a representative of an appropriate body, in a manner consistent with the procedural rules of national law.

Under these provisions, therefore, all children who are capable of expressing a view have a right to do so and to have it taken into account. While these provisions seem straightforward, a careful reading reveals some of the problems associated with the idea of children having a right to participate. Some of these are a direct consequence of the pervasive impact of **developmental psychology** on adult thinking about the **age** at which children become competent to make decisions. For example, adults may allow some children to participate and to express their views in relation to matters that might affect them while excluding others on the grounds that they are incapable of forming their own views or that they are of insufficient age or **maturity**. Since children's **competence** in such situations is determined by adults, meaningful participation, which allows children to make a substantive contribution that affects the outcome of decision-making processes, is easily denied them by deploying such developmentally-based criteria. This is graphically illustrated by Hart's (1997) 'ladder of participation', which identifies a range of modes of participation. These range from 'manipulation' on the first rung of the ladder – in which adults consciously use children's voices to carry their own messages – to 'child-initiated' participation at the top of the ladder. Here children and young people have the ideas, set up the project, and invite adults to join with them in making decisions.

Although devised to analyse children's participation in community development projects, the ladder of participation is a useful device for exploring the nature, extent and impact of children's participation in a much wider range of decision-making processes. This is an important task since most governments are now under an obligation to ensure the participation of children in a wide range of policy issues that will affect their futures as a result of their commitments under the UNCRC. The extent to which any such participation is meaningful in terms of affecting outcomes, however, needs close and careful analysis (see James and James, 2008).

We should also note that Article 12 does not restrict the expression of views to formal language, since children can express their views in a wide variety of ways; for example, through emotions, drawing, painting, singing or drama. Indeed, even very young children, or children with learning difficulties, are capable of expressing views (Lansdown, 2005). Thus the issues to be addressed in considering the extent of children's participation include the ways in which they can be enabled

participation

to participate, the provision of information on which to base their decisions, and the determination of the weight that should be given to the views they do express. Childhood studies therefore has an important contribution to make in relation to each of these.

It is also important to consider the provisions of Article 12 in the context of the nature of the rights they appear to give to children. As it makes clear, such rights have to be understood and located in the context of the procedural rules of national law. In other words, until such time as the provisions of the UNCRC are incorporated into the national law of those States that are party to the Convention, the right to participate, along with all of the other rights contained in the UNCRC, is not enforceable by law.

The contribution of childhood studies to this debate about children's participation has been significant, shedding light not only on children's ability to participate (i.e. their competence to do so) but also the ways in which they exercise their **agency** by participating in a wide variety of settings, the extent to which they participate, the terms on which they do so, and their experiences of both being able to participate and being prevented from participating (Percy-Smith and Thomas, 2010). Thus there is now a substantial body of research that sheds light on, for example, children's participation in **health** care and medical decision making (Alderson, 1993); in relation to **schooling** and education (Alderson, 2000); in the context of **family** breakdown, divorce and post-divorce family life (McNamee et al., 2004; Smart et al., 2001); and in day-to-day decision making in the context of ordinary family life (Butler et al., 2005). Such research makes a rich contribution to the thinking about the nature and extent of children's participation.

FURTHER READING

Alderson, P. (1993) *Children's Consent to Surgery*. Buckingham: Open University Press.

Alderson, P. (2000) 'School students' views on school councils and daily life at school', *Children and Society*, 14(2): 121–35.

Butler, I., Robinson, M. and Scanlan, L. (2005) *Children and Decision Making*. London/York: NCB/JRF.

Cimmens, D. and West, A. (2004) *Having Their Say – Young People and Participation: European experiences*. Lyme Regis: Russell House.

Hart, R. (1997) *Children's Participation: The Theory and Practice of Involving Young Citizens in Community Development and Environmental Care*. London: Earthscan/UNICEF.

James, A.L. and James, A. (2008) 'Changing childhood in the UK: Reconstructing discourses of "risk" and "protection"', in A. James and A.L. James (eds), *European Childhoods: Cultures, Politics and Childhoods in Europe*. London: Palgrave.

Lansdown, G. (2005) *The Evolving Capacities of the Child*. Florence: UNICEF Innocenti Research Centre/Save the Children.

McNamee, S., James, A.L. and James, A. (2004) 'Family law and the construction of childhood in England and Wales', in J. Goddard, A. James and S. McNamee (eds), *The Politics of Childhood: International Perspectives, Contemporary Developments*. London: Palgrave Macmillan.

Percy-Smith, B. and Thomas, N. (eds) (2010) A *Handbook of Children and Young People's Participation: Perspectives from Theory and Practice*. London: Routledge.

Smart, C., Neale, B. and Wade, A. (2001) *The Changing Experience of Childhood*. Cambridge: Polity.

Thomas, N. (2002) *Children, Family and the State: Decision-Making and Child Participation*. Bristol: The Policy Press.

Peer Group

A group of equals, defined in terms of either social status or age.

Used in its literal sense, the concept of an individual having or belonging to a peer group can be applied at any point in the life-course since, sociologically speaking, each and every one of us can be defined or our social status located in terms of certain criteria (educational background, income, occupational status or other indicators of social status) that we share with others and which therefore make them our peers. In this sense the peer group, as a group of people with certain shared characteristics (a *secondary* group), need not be and may never become a face-to-face group (also referred to as *primary* groups), although many primary groups in social life are also peer groups.

The term is most commonly used in relation to children and young people, with particular reference to **youth** groups. This is partly because of the significance of the element of **age** in defining the nature of a peer group and the relatively high visibility of the various styles, cultures and social practices associated with young people, whose tastes, attitudes and behaviours are commonly ascribed by adults to peer-group influence. Such youth cultures have increasingly been linked to patterns of youth consumption that have become central in the production of youthful subjectivities and identities (France, 2007). In this sense, as with adult peer groups, the group need not be a primary group and the notion of peer-group influence simply acknowledges the significance of the social influence of other young people and youth culture as a major point of reference for children and young people during the years of adolescence.

The concept of the peer group also has particular associations with young people, however, because of the perceived significance of the peer group, not only developmentally but also socially, in the lives of both adults and young people. In developmental terms, the period of adolescence is, inter alia, a period in which young people progressively move away from the confines of the family into the broader social world, increasingly exchanging the emotional and social supports previously provided by the family for those provided both by **friendships** with individuals and by friendship groups comprising the young person's peers. Such groups are also important in terms of the **socialisation** process, however, since important learning about the nature and significance of social norms, which influence young people towards uniformity, conformity and obedience, takes place in the context of the peer group (Nicolson et al., 2006).

In many societies, peer groups are heavily based on **gender** and, in developing countries, this often reflects the different forms of economic activity that young people are expected to engage in as **working children** when they reach adolescence. Similarly, the age-sets that are formed in some African societies during the transition to adulthood make the peer group of such considerable social and economic importance that it continues to be of social significance throughout adult life. In industrialised western societies, however, the significance of primary peer groups formed during adolescence tends to wane with the assumption of adult roles and responsibilities.

Young people's peer groups are also important socially, however, not least because of their increasing visibility as young people enter the social world and seek to occupy the same public spaces as adults. But, as with much else in **childhood studies**, there are significant variations in the ways in which this transition from childhood to adulthood is thought about and managed in different social and cultural contexts. In western industrialised societies, for example, peer group pressures have often been seen negatively as the source of deviant behaviours, such as truancy (Nicolson et al., 2006) and more serious forms of **delinquency**.

Matza, for example, observed that 'the situation in which the delinquent is among his [*sic*] peers committing delinquencies, exaggerating, recounting or planning them ... is a view of delinquents within their primary group context on which many observers have almost completely focused' (1964: 51). Nor is this just a recent phenomenon (Pearson, 1983). One consequence of this, particularly in the western world, is that the peer groups of young people have often become the target of a wide range of adult social control measures.

However, the peer group can also be seen in a more positive light. One of the many important contributions made by childhood studies to understanding children and childhood comes from research into the **social worlds** children construct with their peers. This work has revealed much about how children's social and cultural practices differ from those of adults and has also shown the extent to which children's peer groups provide an important social context for children through which they are able to demonstrate and/or receive confirmation of particular social **competences.** For example, as Buckingham and Bragg (2005) have observed, while there remains considerable moral panic about children and young people's access to sexual knowledge via the media, the peer group can provide a space within which children and young people self-regulate their access to and acquisition of what they consider to be 'appropriate' information for their **age-group.** Thus, while 'peer group influence' is often regarded negatively by adults, it can also provide the arena within which children and young people offer help and support to each other that are lacking in their relationships with adults.

FURTHER READING

Buckingham, D. and Bragg, S. (2005) 'Opting into (and out of) childhood: Young people, sex and the media', in J. Qvortrup (ed.), *Studies in Modern Childhood: Society, Agency and Culture.* Basingstoke: Palgrave Macmillan.

France, A. (2007) *Understanding Youth in Late Modernity.* Maidenhead: Open University Press/ McGraw-Hill Education.

Matza, D. (1964) *Delinquency and Drift.* New York: Wiley.

Nicolson, P., Boyne, R. and Owen, J. (2006) *Applied Psychology for Social Workers.* Basingstoke: Palgrave Macmillan.

Pearson, G. (1983) *Hooligan: A History of Respectable Fears.* London: Macmillan.

> *Pleasurable activities freely engaged in by children; freedom from **work**; to act frivolously or capriciously.*

The above definitions of play, as both verb and noun, are the ones usually to be found in the dictionary, and for Huizinga (1949), an early theorist of play, the term refers to activities that are outside of the ordinary run of everyday life. Though not serious, they are utterly absorbing to the player. Characterised by pleasure and seen as an end in itself, play, Huizinga says, has its own rules of engagement and comes to constitute a separate world apart from the humdrum everyday world.

However, while this account of play can be useful to describe some adult activities – as in 'playing' sports, such as tennis or football – as a key concept of **childhood studies**, these descriptions do not suffice. Indeed, they are potentially misleading since they contain a range of assumptions about both the quality and content of the activity described as play, assumptions that stem from an adult perspective rather than from children's **standpoint**.

It is, however, surprisingly difficult to provide a child-focused definition of play since, in part, 'play' is defined by its opposite: **work**. Work describes activities that are not only serious, effortful and usually carried out for monetary gain, but these activities also carry with them restrictive obligations of different kinds. It is for these reasons that 'play', when used in relation to adult activities, necessarily gives rise to ideas of fun, pleasure, amusement, frivolity and freedom – qualities that are the exact opposite of work. However, since children are in part defined by their very difference from adults, we might expect 'play', when seen as a children's activity, to take on rather different qualities.

From the perspective of child development, play has traditionally been made to carry an immense purposeful load for children as it is through play, for example, that children are said to learn (Bruner et al., 1976). Play is thus regarded as a key part of children's activities and as an essential aspect of **childhood**, with play theorists highlighting the numerous important functions that play performs in children's development. For example, play offers scope for role learning through mimicry; play provides opportunities for cognitive problem solving; it has an important role in developing motor skills; and it provides exercise, improving **health** and providing opportunities for forging **friendships** and other social relationships. Indeed, Article 31 of the United Nations Convention on the Rights of the Child (**UNCRC**) 1989 explicitly recognises the 'right of the child to rest and leisure, to engage in play and recreational activities'. In the childhood context, then, play appears to lose some of its associations with freedom and spontaneity and becomes a more obligatory activity for children. Indeed, those children who are not able to play are seen to be at risk of impoverished social and cognitive development. 'Go out to play!' adults cry – this is what children are supposed to do.

From a childhood studies perspective, however, play has to be seen in a much broader context. Thus, for example, while distinctions are sometimes drawn between free, imaginative play and more formalised rule-bound games, such as Hide and Seek or Tig (Opie and Opie, 1969), the virtues of these different play forms are debated in terms of what role these play in children's lives. Schwartzman's early (1978) analysis showed that play of all kinds is integral to children's **social worlds** and to the ways in which children make use of the different **spaces** in the environment. As later researchers have continued to document, it provides the medium through which children's friendships and peer cultures are facilitated and is a key context for the process of **interpretive reproduction** – that which enables children to learn about the social world.

The extent to which play facilitates the expression of **gender** differences during childhood has been the subject of debate. Early work by Lever (1978) suggested, for instance, that girls' games encourage co-operation rather than competition, providing each gender with different skills for later life. Goodwin's more recent work, however, argues against those who have suggested that girls' games lack the 'intellectual complexity and intricate division of labour' that are said to be char-acteristic of boys' play (Goodwin, 2006: 34). In her analysis of girls playing the game of Hopscotch in a North American playground, she shows how keen the girls are to spot and call out the mistakes that others make, since this will enable them to get a chance to play the game. Moreover, she shows that, despite stereo-types of Latina girls as being 'the hapless victims of a patriarchal culture', they are just as vocal in demanding their turn as their English-speaking counterparts (2006: 72). As Goodwin shows, the games girls play can involve conflict as well as co-operation and therefore these offer 'rich possibilities for cognitive organisa-tion and display of powerful stances [that] are embedded within a larger ethos of playfulness' (2006: 67).

From the perspective of childhood studies, play is a key concept not only because it is so heavily implicated in definitions of childhood and 'the child', but also because, so often, children's play provides one of the most important contexts for **child-focused research** that enables insight into the social worlds of children.

FURTHER READING

Bruner, J.S., Jolly, A. and Sylva, K. (1976) *Play: Its Role in Development and Evolution*. Harmondsworth: Penguin.

Goodwin, M.H. (2006) *The Hidden Life of Girls*. Oxford: Blackwell.

Huizinga, J. (1949) *Homo Ludens: A Study of the Play-Element in Culture*. London: Routledge & Kegan Paul.

Lanclos, D.M. (2003) *At Play in Belfast*. Camden, NJ: Rutgers University Press.

Lever, J. (1978) 'Sex differences in the complexity of children's play and games', *American Sociological Review*, 43: 471–83.

Opie, I. and Opie, P. (1969) *Children's Games in Street and Playground*. Oxford: Clarendon.

Schwartzman, H.B. (1978) *Transformations: The Anthropology of Children's Play*. New York: Plenum.

key concepts in
childhood studies

The rate of child poverty is now commonly accepted to be the proportion of children living in families that have only 60 per cent of the median national income before housing costs are met.

The apparent simplicity of this definition conceals a debate that has preoccupied social policy analysts for many years. It is a debate that has particular significance for making international comparisons since national median incomes, and therefore the embedded quality of life issues, vary enormously among countries and their economies. This is a result of variations in gross domestic product (GDP), which is a powerful determinant of the median income level of any given population. The adoption of a definition of relative (as opposed to absolute) poverty is therefore seen by many as the only way to make international comparisons, in spite of the fact that such comparisons inevitably conceal major differences in lifestyle and the quality of life in different societies.

The weakness of this approach, according to its critics, is that 'relative poverty is not "real" poverty' (UNICEF, 2007), since many of those who fall below relative poverty lines in advanced western economies currently enjoy a standard of living that is higher than at any time in the past. It is certainly much better than that of most of the world's children who live in the majority South. While this is undoubtedly the case, what this criticism fails to acknowledge is the *experience* of poverty that comes from the day-to-day exposure to the differences between the lives of those living in poverty and the lives of others around them.

It is also important to recognise the links between poverty and social stratification, whether these are based on social class, educational background, caste or any other form of structurally-based differentiation between social groups, since in the large majority of societies the distribution of income reflects such structural inequalities, regardless of GDP, and they can therefore be said also to 'cause' poverty.

Poverty is by no means a concept that is unique to childhood studies; it is an issue that bears down across **generations** and affects the quality of life of young and old alike. It is of particular importance in relation to children and young people, however, for a number of reasons. For example, in the developed countries of Europe, almost every aspect of children's **health** and **welfare** is affected by poverty: rates of sickness and mortality; incidence of mental health problems; quality of housing and education; involvement in crime and **delinquency**; and employment prospects. Indeed, it is hard to think of any aspect of childhood that is not negatively affected by the presence of poverty, with all that this implies in terms of social exclusion (Bradshaw and Mayhew, 2005; Jensen and Qvortrup, 2004).

Although poverty defined in this way is therefore one of the most pervasive negative influences on children's well-being, it must also be considered in relation to other structural factors such as **generation**. For example, are children 'richer' or 'poorer' than other age groups? Is the distribution of income between children and the elderly population changing and, if so, what are the implications of this (Jensen and Qvortrup, 2004)?

Such analyses highlight the fact that relatively little is known officially about children's economic circumstances or activities; for example, how many children are in paid employment; how much do they earn; what hours do they **work**; what do they spend their earnings on? Partly because such data are not collected by governments, the conventional view, certainly with regard to western societies, is that the activities of **working children** are of only marginal economic importance. However, this is because much of the work that children do goes unrecorded and often unregulated, which in turn raises important questions about the impact this has on the quality of children's lives. In other words, the relationship between child work and poverty is something we know very little about, because children do not figure in official data about levels of economic activity. This lack of information is not only important in itself, it is important for what it signifies: that children's experience of poverty can only be inferred from measures of the poverty of their parents and the households in which they live. This symbolically locates children firmly within the framework of the **family**, reinforcing their status as dependants and obscuring their **agency**, both economically and socially.

What such definitions and discourses also exclude, therefore, are children's *experiences* of poverty, yet what comparative data we do have (see, for example, Jensen and Qvortrup, 2004; UNICEF, 2007) suggest that the impact of poverty on children's lives can vary enormously, even within the relatively advanced economies of Europe. In Croatia, for example, where 80 per cent of Croats consider themselves to be poor, it is the experience of social exclusion arising from poverty, rather than physical deprivation, that was considered most important by children: not being able to afford to go out or to buy new clothes; eating a monotonous diet; insufficient money to travel from the countryside into the city. Ridge's (2002) exploration of children's perspective on poverty in the UK offers comparable insights into the feelings of exclusion that poverty can bring. Through **child-focused research**, she showed that poor children felt excluded from **participation** in such things as school trips, and she highlighted the humiliation many felt at having to have free school meals. The accounts of children growing up in poverty in the majority South – where children's work is a fact of life for the majority of poor families since their economic survival may depend on the work that children do – present an altogether different picture of the experience of poverty (Montgomery et al., 2003).

The United Nations Convention on the Rights of the Child (**UNCRC**) 1989 calls for the creation of circumstances that will ensure 'the right of the child to the enjoyment of the highest attainable standard of health', which includes taking measures to diminish infant and child mortality (Article 24); that will provide the right to 'a standard of living adequate for the child's physical, mental, spiritual moral and social development' (Article 27); that will provide for the education of the child in order to allow 'the development of the child's personality, talents and mental and physical abilities to their fullest potential' (Article 29); that will recognise the right of the child 'to rest and leisure, to engage in play and recreational activities' (Article 31); and that will protect the child 'from economic exploitation and from performing any work that is likely to be hazardous or to interfere with the child's education' (Article 32). Thus poverty also goes to the heart of many of the provisions of the UNCRC and the struggle for its full implementation, hence its particular importance in the context of childhood studies.

FURTHER READING

Boyden, J., Ling, B. and Myers, W. (1998) *What Works for Working Children*. Stockholm: Save the Children.

Bradshaw, J. and Mayhew, E. (eds) (2005) *The Well-being of Children in the UK* (2nd edn). London: Save the Children.

Jensen, A. and Qvortrup, J. (2004) 'Summary – A childhood mosaic: What did we learn', in A-M. Jensen, A. Ben-Arieh, C. Conti, D. Kutsar, M.N.G. Phádraig and H.W. Nielsen (eds), *Children's Welfare in Ageing Europe*, Vols I and II. Trondheim: NOSEB.

Montgomery, H., Burr, R. and Woodhead, M. (2003) *Changing Childhoods: Local and Global*. Milton Keynes/Chichester: Open University Press/Wiley.

Penn, H. (2002) 'The World Bank's view of early childhood', *Childhood*, 9(1): 118–32.

Ridge, T. (2002) *Childhood Poverty and Social Exclusion: From a Child's Perspective*. Bristol: The Policy Press.

UNICEF (2007) *Child Poverty in Perspective: An Overview of Child Well-being in Rich Countries*. Innocenti Report Card 7, UNICEF Innocenti Research Centre. Florence: United Nations Children's Fund.

Protection

'Child protection' is a term applied to the protection of children of all ages by the State and its agents from deliberate or inadvertent harm, most usually but not exclusively in the context of family relations.

For as far back as we have historical records, there is evidence that children in different parts of the world have suffered a range of hardships, which many would now define as abuse, at the hands of adults and adult society. This ranges from forms of culturally sanctioned practices such as female genital mutilation, economically sanctioned practices concerning child labour, ethnically sanctioned practices such as the kidnapping of children from different tribal groups, and practices that have combined these elements, such as child slavery.

It is only the relatively recent 'discovery' of **childhood** as a distinct social and developmental phase in the life-course, which has justified the development and introduction of policies aimed specifically at the particular and distinct needs of children as a social group, that perspectives on such practices have begun to alter. As children have increasingly been seen as not only needing but also deserving special measures to protect them from such adversities, so we have seen the emergence of 'child protection' in the latter part of the 20th century as a concept with very specific meanings. Initially focused on physical abuse (the so-called 'battered baby syndrome') the focus of concern over the maltreatment of children has subsequently broadened to include emotional abuse, **neglect** and **sexual abuse**.

Child protection has therefore come to signify the need for children to be protected by the State from a range of types of maltreatment by adults, which can be both active and passive. Thus, for example, active abuse can involve non-accidental physical abuse, psychological violence such as intimidation or other forms of emotional abuse, and sexual violence such as incest, sexual assault and rape. Similarly, passive abuse can involve physical neglect or poor health care, the psychological damage caused by emotional neglect, or lack of affection, and sexual abuse such as the failure to protect a child from abuse by others, including prostitution.

At the same time, however, particularly within western industrialised countries, this developing concern with children's protection has, paradoxically, produced a narrowing of perspective, tending to concentrate focus on the protection of children from abuse within the **family**. It is only relatively recently that, in the UK for example, this has begun to widen out into the broader concept of 'safeguarding' children more generally. This marked political shift signifies a redefinition of the range and extent of risks against which children need to be protected.

Although abuse in the family is still an important area of concern, the redefinition of risk means that children are now seen in the UK as needing to be safeguarded against a broader range of adversities in their lives as children, which could have a negative impact on their lives as adults. This includes risks to their physical and mental health from smoking, obesity and teenage pregnancy; the need to stay safe from harm and neglect; the need to develop the skills necessary for adulthood through maximising educational participation and achievement; the risk of becoming involved in offending and not becoming fully contributing members of society, not only socially but also economically and politically; and the risk of not overcoming socio-economic disadvantages and achieving their full potential in adult life. Thus, the concept of safeguarding has introduced a much wider range of risks against which children need to be protected as part of ensuring their **welfare**.

This shift of emphasis has been due in part to the **rights** given to children under the United Nations Convention of the Rights of the Child (**UNCRC**) 1989. Although these cover the entire range of children's needs and aspirations, including conventional civil and political rights, the Convention also contains a lengthy list of what have been referred to as 'protection rights'. These not only require those States who have signed up to the Convention to protect children from all forms of abuse in the context of the family, but also to protect them in a range of other contexts: for example, from sexual abuse, exploitation and prostitution; from the harmful effects of child **work**; from any excesses by the State in terms of the punishment of juvenile offenders; and from various aspects of armed conflict, including direct participation in hostilities as **child soldiers** and ensuring the provision of humanitarian assistance for refugee children.

Thus, by virtue of including children's social, economic and welfare rights, 'the Convention also emphasises that States must not only protect children and safeguard their fundamental freedoms, but also devote resources to ensuring that they realise their potential for maturing into healthy and happy adulthood' (Fortin, 2003: 37). With the near universal adoption of the UNCRC, attention has therefore begun to focus once more not only on abuse in the family but also on the many abuses that take place outside it.

Whether cast in terms of protection or safeguarding, the discourses surrounding both the maltreatment of children and the need to provide them with safe, secure and well-resourced environments in which they can develop into healthy and happy adults underline an issue of fundamental interest to childhood studies: by casting children's rights primarily in the context of protection and welfare, the basic ordering of relationships between the State and the family and between adults and children, and the dependence of the latter on the former, is reinforced. It is adults, through the State and the family, who are charged with protecting and safeguarding children, with making decisions in children's **best interests**, and who are responsible for ensuring that children's rights are provided for.

While the contribution of the UNCRC to the increased international awareness of the need for child protection is clearly to be welcomed, one of its weaknesses lies in its failure to acknowledge the capacities of children and their ability to contribute to their own welfare. There is, for example, an increasing body of evidence 'that children are capable of exercising **agency** and utilising their own resources and strengths in developing strategies for their protection ... [p]rotective approaches that make children dependent on adult support leave children without resources when those adult protections are withdrawn' (Lansdown, 2006: 147).

Thus there is a dissonance between, on the one hand, the struggle and achievements of **childhood studies** to recognise and make explicit the agency of children, with all that this implies about their **competence**, their **participation** rights in terms of their being involved in making decisions that affect them, and their lack of **citizenship** status; and on the other, the importance of the rights of children under the UNCRC, which emphasises their need for protection, their dependence upon adults and therefore, implicitly at least, their lack of competence. In this sense, there is a tension in the otherwise close affinity between childhood studies and the children's rights movement. This tension will continue as long as children are not constructed as autonomous rights holders, with the consequent right of being able to enforce and secure their own rights, including their rights to protection, independent of adults.

protection

FURTHER READING

Fortin, J. (2003) *Children's Rights and the Developing Law* (2nd edn). London: LexisNexis/ Butterworths.

Lansdown, G. (2006) 'International developments in children's participation: Lessons and challenges', in K. Tisdall, J. Davis, M. Hill and A. Prout (eds), *Children, Young People and Social Inclusion*. Bristol: The Policy Press.

Myers, W. and Boyden, J. (2001) *Strengthening Children in Situations of Adversity*. Oxford: Refugee Studies Centre.

Wilson, K. and James, A.L. (eds) (2007) *The Child Protection Handbook: The Practitoner's Guide to Safeguarding Children* (3rd edn). Edinburgh: Ballière Tindall/Elsevier.

Representation

> *The linguistic or figurative process by which ideas are given significance and meaning in society.*

The process of representing **childhood** is core to understanding the different ways in which children are understood in different societies and also, therefore, to the different everyday lives that they experience. Representations, according to Hall (1997), are key to meaning making, forming a systematic set of ideas that contribute to the ongoing **social construction** of reality. And because sets of representations are therefore always located in particular cultures or historical moments (or otherwise how else would they be meaningful?) we have to think about them as part of what Foucault (1972) terms a *discourse*. That is to say, taken together, a set of representations becomes a way of thinking or talking about the world; it provides a frame through which we see the world in particular ways.

In relation to children and childhood, understanding the power that these discourses, or sets of representations, can have is important because they shape children's everyday lives and experiences. In relation to the kinds of language associated with the idea of 'the child' and 'childhood' James et al. (1998), for example, show the ways in which different historical representations have recurred over time and have been highly influential in shaping social attitudes and practices towards children. Thus, for example, the idea that children are born **innocent** has its roots in the representations of childhood to be found in the 18th-century writings of Jean Jacques Rousseau, who rejected the earlier Puritan ideas that children were born inherently evil. Represented as, by nature, sinful, children in the 16th and 17th centuries were subjected to harsh regimes of discipline so that goodness, next to godliness, might be encouraged.

Exploring contemporary representations of children and childhood, this tension between the innocent and the sinful child recurs in, for example, the different and changing ways in which children and young people who come into conflict with the law are defined and then treated within the criminal justice system. Under some government regimes, young children are represented as not responsible for their actions, leading to a **welfare** approach being adopted, in which context children may receive help and assistance to overcome their difficulties. Elsewhere, the call is for their punishment and control, so that children might be taught a lesson and learn to alter their behaviour.

By contrast, Castañeda (2002) shows how it is the unfinished nature of the child's body that leaves it open to a wide range of medical and scientific representations transnationally, representations that undoubtedly can have very powerful consequences for children themselves through the workings of the **cultural politics of childhood**.

Turning to more figurative representations of childhood, as Holland (2006) observes, in the contemporary modern world, images of children abound and those that appear on television and bill-board advertisements draw on many of the 'ideologies which have attached themselves to childhood, playfulness, innocence and victimisation' (2006: 2). These, she argues, constitute narratives about childhood that attempt to fix its meaning but which also leave open the possibility for the negotiation of new or different meanings, depending upon the social contexts in which they are used.

Representations are also important in **childhood studies** since, as we have defined it as a multi-disciplinary endeavour, it opens up for consideration the many and varied ways in which different disciplines represent children, for different disciplinary purposes and to different audiences. Thus, as implied above, historical accounts reflect different representations of children and childhood in different eras; economic accounts engage in the debate about the role of children as consumers and as a source of labour; literary accounts explore, amongst other things, the ontology of childhood; while legal discourse considers the role of the child in the very specific context of law and social regulation.

FURTHER READING

Castañeda, C. (2002) *Figurations*. Durham, NC: Duke University Press.
Chin, S.E. (2008) *Inventing Modern Adolescence*. Camden, NJ: Rutgers University Press.
Foucault, M. (1972) *The Archaeology of Knowledge*. London: Tavistock.
Hall, S. (ed.) (1997) *Representation: Cultural Representations and Signifying Practices*. London: Sage.
Holland, P. (2006) *Picturing Childhood: The Myth of the Child in Popular Imagery*. London: Tauris.
James, A., Jenks, C. and Prout, A. (1998) *Theorizing Childhood*. Cambridge: Polity.
Murdoch, L. (2006) *Imagined Orphans: Poor Families, Child-welfare, Contested Citizenship in London, 1870–1918*. Camden, NJ: Rutgers University Press.

Resilience

An unevenly distributed variable of behavioural and emotional functioning that enables children and young people (and adults) differentially to cope with, and adapt positively to, adverse circumstances and experiences, thereby ameliorating to various degrees their negative effects and enabling positive adjustments to be made, even in conditions of risk.

As a concept applied to children and young people, resilience has perhaps emerged from, and been most prominent in, discourses about child abuse and **protection**. It has become more important in the context of **childhood studies**, however, because of the opportunity it offers to focus on children's **agency**, their adaptive and coping abilities and their **competence**, in contrast to dominant adult discourses that tend to focus on their **vulnerability** and need for protection.

Affected by both personality and environmental factors, resilience should be considered as a process or a phenomenon rather than as a personality characteristic of an individual. Resilience is associated with having a good sense of self-efficacy, and self-esteem and ego strength, giving the ability to make choices and exercise a degree of control. The attributes of each **child** in terms of intelligence, temperament and coping skills are also important. However, such characteristics are a product not only of the wider environment in which a child is raised and the experiences to which they are exposed, including the impact of factors such as **poverty**; they are also associated with the formation of secure emotional attachments in early life (particularly with mothers), with positive family functioning, and with having and using social support when needed. Thus, important risk modifiers are the attributes of an individual child, the influence of their **family**, and the social and community context in which they live. The production of resilience therefore reflects a complex individual and social process involving the interaction of a wide range of variables.

In considering the way in which resilience operates as a variable, it is important to note that the *absence* of factors that research has shown to be associated with risk, vulnerabilities and poor outcomes for some children (e.g. having a teenage mother, or a parent with mental health or substance misuse problems) does not necessarily result in particularly positive outcomes for a child. In addition, there is an important debate amongst researchers about the extent to which the presence of resilience based on the development of such attributes can be seen as a positive outcome of exposure to such risks, or a pre-existing protective factor; in its absence, an aspect of a child's vulnerability; or whether these are two sides of the same coin. There is also a degree of uncertainty about the extent to which the possession of resilience, or competence in coping with risks, is related to competence more generally.

It is difficult to analyse and measure the concept of resilience without also considering how we define and understand the concepts of risk and vulnerability, and how this translates into our understanding, identification and definition of threats to children, not least because these are to some considerable extent culturally and politically defined. Not only do the construction and understanding of risks vary between cultures and contexts, they also vary historically within cultures, depending upon varying political and social sensibilities. This is clearly demonstrated, for example, by the shifting parameters of the debate about child abuse and protection within the UK, and the ways in which children's **responsibilities** are defined (Evans and Becker, 2009).

Importantly, the risk and resilience paradigms embody different assumptions about and constructions of behaviour and adaptation to environmental pressures: risk research focuses on negative outcomes, while resilience research focuses on the positive and negative aspects of both outcomes and predisposing factors. The advantage of the positive focus that is provided by the concept of resilience in studying and understanding children and young people is that it encourages adults to consider children's agency (their strengths, abilities and competences) when faced with difficult circumstances, rather than focusing on their weaknesses, vulnerabilities and dependency. In their study of children acting as carers for parents with HIV/AIDS in the UK and in Tanzania, Evans and Becker (2009) demonstrate the different and complex ways in which children's resilience is fostered in these often difficult circumstances.

Even a brief consideration of the research on **street children** illustrates some of these issues: compare, for example, the variable numbers of such children in different countries, and the varying degrees of adult acceptance of, and State concern about, the circumstances in which such children live. Consider, too, the research evidence about the resilience of such children, sometimes living in very challenging circumstances, and their ability to develop subcultures that provide a sense of belonging and a positive self-image, both of which are associated with the development of resilience.

The importance of the notion of resilience also lies in the fact that it requires us to focus on the individual child rather than children in general, their particular circumstances, and their unique selves and coping abilities. Resilience cautions against viewing all children faced with a particular set of negative life-circumstances as a homogeneous group by alerting us to the need to take into account their individuality, in terms of both intrinsic and extrinsic variables, that can moderate the risks to which they are exposed. The downside of this process of individualisation, however, is that it can result in a degree of blame and **responsibility** being attached to those who do not cope so well.

FURTHER READING

Daniel, B., Wassell, S. and Gilligan, R. (1999) *Child Development for Child Care and Protection Workers*. London: Jessica Kingsley. (See especially Ch. 4, 'Resilience and Vulnerability'.)

Evans, R. and Becker, S. (2009) *Children Caring for Parents with HIV/AIDS: Global Issues and Policy Responses*. Bristol: The Policy Press.

James, A.L. and James, A. (2008) 'Changing childhood in the UK: reconstructing discourses of "risk" and "protection"', in A. James and A.L. James (eds), *European Childhoods: Cultures, Politics and Childhoods in Europe*. Basingstoke: Palgrave Macmillan.

Luthar, S.S. (ed.) (2003) *Resilience and Vulnerability*. New York: Cambridge University Press.

Parton, N. (2006) *Safeguarding Childhood: Early Intervention and Surveillance in a Late Modern Society*. Basingstoke: Palgrave Macmillan.

Rutter, M. (2000) 'Resilience reconsidered: Conceptual considerations, empirical findings, and policy implications', in J.P. Shonkoff and S.J. Meisels (eds), *Handbook of Early Childhood Intervention* (2nd edn). Cambridge: Cambridge University Press.

Wilson, K. and James, A.L. (eds) (2007) *The Child Protection Handbook*. London/Edinburgh: Elsevier/Ballière-Tindall.

resilience

> *A deceptively simple concept implying accountability to someone for something but one that has considerable rhetorical power, in the various contexts in which it is used and the meanings that it is given, in discourses about childhood.*

To have a responsibility for something, whether it be for discharging a duty to complete a task or fulfilling a role, is to be accountable for any failure to meet that responsibility. That accountability may be towards an individual, such as a friend or a parent; it may be towards an institution such as a school, an employer or, on a larger social scale, the State; it may be towards a community, as in the case of a political, religious, secular, social or geographical community; or it may be a towards something altogether more abstract, such as or a set of beliefs or values. In each case, the meeting of that responsibility leads to certain rewards: these may be material rewards; social approval or approbation leading to support, acceptance and social integration; or rewards in terms of social status and **rights**.

The failure to accept (i.e. to agree to be responsible for something) or to meet a responsibility therefore implies the imposition of sanctions. These mirror the rewards that are offered: that is, the loss of material rewards or the imposition of financial penalties, the loss of social status or approval, or, in the case of a failure to meet moral standards, an internalised sense of failure to live up to a desired standard. Indeed, a failure to live up to one's responsibilities as a citizen towards the State can result in loss of rights, liberty or the imposition of physical punishment. It is clear from this that the concept of responsibility is central to the process of **socialisation**, whereby children are taught and learn to conform to the expectations of their parents, their **family**, their community and society more generally.

Responsibility is therefore of particular importance in relation to debates about children and **childhood** because it is something that is widely seen as a social commodity that, as far as children are concerned, is in the gift of adults. In the case of being given an unpleasant job or household chore to do, it may be an imposition for some children, whereas the same task in a different cultural context may represent a gift leading to the enhanced social status that comes from making a valued contribution to a collective social unit such as the **family** or **peer group**.

It follows from this that responsibility can be regarded, inter alia, as an important nexus (one of many) between the worlds of adults and children. If responsibility, in most contexts, is something that is directly allocated or socially ascribed to children by adults, it becomes a powerful symbol of adult–**child** relations. Of necessity, it embodies and reflects a wide range of assumptions and adult judgements concerning childhood and children about **age**, maturity and **competence**. Such assumptions are deeply embedded in these relations as they are variously constructed in different cultural and political contexts. Without such assumptions being made, the basis on which children and young people are, at various points and stages in their lives, deemed to be capable of being allocated and taking responsibility for certain roles and tasks, and being competent to discharge the responsibilities involved in them, would be purely arbitrary. Therefore, the way in which any given society understands and defines the responsibilities that should be given to children, including any inconsistencies and ambiguities that might be observed in this process, reveals important dimensions of both the **cultural politics** and the **social construction** of childhood, and very real insights into the nature and fabric **generational** relations and the rhetorical strategies used to support these.

As we have argued elsewhere (James and James, 2004), law plays an important role in the structuring of such relations, including the formal allocation of rights and responsibilities to both adults and children. Therefore it is instructive to observe, for example, that in England and Wales the law regards the responsibility of children very differently in different contexts. Thus, in spite of recommendations to the contrary from the UN Committee on the Rights of the Child, in 1998, the government effectively lowered the **age** in criminal proceedings at which a child can be held to be responsible for their behaviour from 14 to 10. In contrast, in divorce proceedings children still have no absolute right to be heard, while courts are reluctant to listen to children's views much below the age of 12 and, in effect, retain the right to disregard their views until the age of 16. This is because they are viewed as lacking in competence and as being too young to be given the responsibility of influencing decisions concerning their future.

Part of the significance of the concept of responsibility in **childhood studies** is that it is also increasingly connected discursively with the issue of rights, both implicitly and explicitly. It has already been noted above that the allocation of rights may be one of the social rewards for the acceptance of responsibilities, but it is also the case that as long as adults construct children as unequal to and dependent upon them, it is problematic for children to be seen as being responsible enough to hold rights. This is illustrated by the example above in which the legal view of children in divorce proceedings defines them as being dependants and therefore dependent, unlike criminal proceedings in which they are viewed as capable of possessing and exercising their **agency,** albeit irresponsibly.

Bearing in mind the centrality of children's agency in childhood studies, this reminds us of the need to acknowledge that children and young people do not always, or necessarily, accept the responsibilities that adults seek to place on them. A common sanction imposed by adults in such circumstances is to withdraw any rights already allocated, or to withhold those not yet allocated. In the UK, for example, the mantra of 'no rights without responsibilities' is one that has been deployed particularly (but by no means exclusively) in relation to children and young people in debates about **citizenship,** and in many countries the label of **delinquency** is a powerful marker of any perceived failure of young people to accept and live up to their legal and/or social responsibilities.

One consequence of this has been increasing political and social pressure on the parents of anti-social and delinquent children to 'take responsibility' for the behaviour of their children, reflecting what has been referred to as a 'responsibilisation strategy' as part of which parents and communities, rather than the State, are expected to take responsibility for the behaviour of children who do not conform to expected standards. The political and social prominence given to such issues in the UK means that, in spite of decades of debate about children's rights since the United Nations Convention on the Rights of the Child (**UNCRC**) 1989 came into effect, children remain highly dependent on adults and continue to be seen in many contexts as lacking responsibility and therefore not capable (or deserving) of being given rights.

FURTHER READING

Cockburn, T. (1998) 'Children and citizenship in Britain', *Childhood*, 5(1): 99–117.

Fortin, J. (2003) *Children's Rights and the Developing Law* (2nd edn). London: LexisNexis.

Freeman, M. (1992) 'Taking children's rights more seriously', in P. Alston, S. Parker and J. Seymour (eds), *Children, Rights and the Law*. Oxford: Clarendon.

James, A. and James, A.L. (2004) *Constructing Childhood: Theory, Policy and Social Practice*. London: Palgrave Macmillan.

James, A.L. (2008) 'Responsibility, children and childhood', in J. Bridgeman, C. Lind and H. Keating (eds), *Responsibility, Law and the Family*. Aldershot: Ashgate.

Muncie, J. (2004) 'Youth justice: Responsibility and rights', in J. Roche, S. Tucker, R. Thomson and R. Flynn (eds), *Youth in Society* (2nd edn). London: Sage.

Rights are claims that are justifiable on legal or moral grounds to have or obtain something, or to act in a certain way. Although the two may often be the same, the existence of a moral right may not necessarily be embodied in a legal right, the enforcement of which can be pursued through the courts or similar tribunals, while a legal right may not necessarily carry much moral weight.

The debate about the nature of rights is complex, raising many difficult philosophical, legal and social issues revolving around the nature and basis of social relationships, as well as the relationship between the individual and the State. Such issues are all the more complex in relation to children, not least because some, influenced by the orthodoxy of **developmental psychology**, would argue that since children are incapable of exercising choice, or at least of doing so with competence, and since by definition they also lack experience, they should not be given **responsibility** as holders of rights. Yet it is not morally defensible, in the context of any organised society or social group, to argue that children as an entire social category not only *do* not but *can* not and *should* not have any rights, for to do so would be to undermine the very nature of social responsibility and relationships. Consequently, it can be argued that a child should and *does* have rights, both legal and moral, but that these need not necessarily be the same as those of adults.

This, in essence, is the thrust of the United Nations Convention on the Rights of the Child (**UNCRC**) 1989, which contains a wide range of provisions relating to the rights of children. Many of these are unique to the particular **needs** of individuals in that phase of the life-course that constitutes **childhood** and are usually described in terms of 'the three ps': rights to provision, **protection** and **participation**. As the preamble to the Convention notes, following the Universal Declaration of Human Rights, 'childhood is entitled to special care and assistance' and 'the child, by reason of his [*sic*] physical and mental immaturity, needs special safeguards and care, including appropriate legal protection'. This makes it clear that the rights of the child under the Convention are related to the special needs associated with childhood as a developmental phase – needs related to protection, to particular provisions such as **schooling** and education, **health** care and **family** life, and to participation. These are rather different from the kinds of positive rights associated with adulthood and the status of **citizenship**.

The UNCRC does something else of considerable importance: it defines a set of rights that, 'having taken due account of the importance of the traditions and cultural values of each people for the protection and harmonious development of the child', are intended to be applied to *all* children, wherever they may be born and wherever they may live. The Convention therefore outlines in its first 40 Articles a set of necessarily generally worded rights that construct a globalised model of childhood.

The UNCRC has therefore been of enormous significance, particularly to the work of the children's rights 'movement', and has triggered an international debate about childhood and the nature of children's rights. By offering such a globalised model of childhood, however, it undermines some of the major advances made by **childhood studies** in recognising the **diversity** of childhoods, since it cannot easily accommodate the fact that children in different parts of the world, in different social and cultural contexts, have very different experiences of being children.

The debate about children's rights has also engendered a degree of opposition from various quarters since they can be viewed as oppositional to parental rights: that is, by giving children rights, it is argued, the authority and **responsibility** of parents are undermined as the family becomes subject to increasing levels of State intervention. It is this view, for example, that is thought to underpin the failure of the USA to ratify the UNCRC. There are also concerns that the currency of children's rights might be devalued by the UNCRC, first by promulgating so many rights, and second by promulgating rights that are so vague that, even if the provisions of the Convention were to be incorporated into either international or domestic law, enforcement would be highly problematic. Thus although the UNCRC apparently 'gives' rights to children, these rights are best understood as moral and aspirational.

Critics would also argue that rights of children under the Convention are further weakened by the mechanisms provided by the UN for their enforcement. Although these require a regular monitoring of States' compliance with the Convention by the responsible UN Committee, this has few effective means of enforcing compliance. Thus, in spite of apparently near universal support for the UNCRC, there are wide variations in the extent to which the rights of children have been achieved.

In addition, it is also clear that any rights of substance are closely related to the issue of citizenship, a status that children acquire only on achieving the age of majority (which varies from country to country). It is only with full citizenship status that full political rights (e.g. the right to vote) are acquired. And in many countries, it is only with citizenship status that an individual is able independently to seek the enforcement of their rights, through the courts or similar tribunals. In other words, even if children are accorded substantive legal rights, there are few situations in which they would be able to seek the enforcement of these without the involvement and support of adults. It is interesting to note that there is nothing inherent in the nature of children's rights that means that this situation is inevitable; for example, the *African Charter on the Rights of the Welfare of the Child*, which addresses children's economic, social, cultural, civil and political rights, contains the right of individual petition for all children (Van Bueren, 1995).

Importantly, however, citizenship (and the cluster of rights and responsibilities associated with it) is about much more than the right to vote: it is about membership of and full participation in a community and, as Archard (2004) notes, it is around this issue that the debates coalesce. On one side are 'the caretakers', who are concerned with ensuring children's rights that will preserve the special status of childhood; on the other side are 'the liberationists', who wish to free children and young people from their marginal status in a world dominated by adults' concerns and agendas, by enabling them to have rights that will facilitate their full membership of society as children and young people.

FURTHER READING

Archard, D. (2004) *Children: Rights and Childhood*. London: Routledge.

Fortin, J. (2003) *Children's Rights and the Developing Law* (2nd edn). London: LexisNexis/ Butterworth.

Franklin, B. (2002) *The New Handbook of Children's Rights*. London: Routledge.

James, A. and James, A.L. (2004) *Constructing Childhood: Theory, Policy and Social Practice*. London: Palgrave Macmillan.

Liebel, M. (2012) *Children's Rights from Below: Cross-Cultural Perspectives*. Basingstoke: Palgrave Macmillan.

Van Bueren, G. (1995) *The International Law on the Rights of the Child*. The Hague: Martinus Nijhoff.

Schooling and Schools

> The process of educating children through the social institution of school and also children's experience of that process.

One of the distinctions that is often drawn between adults and children is that adults have to go to **work** and children have to go to school. However, as research on **working children** shows, this distinction certainly does not apply for the majority of the world's children, and even in modern industrialised societies many children also work. Nonetheless, it remains the case that an important landmark in the development of modern conceptions of childhood was the withdrawal of children from the labour force and the making of school attendance compulsory. In England, this process took place in the 1870s and 1880s and, as Hendrick comments, 'the significance of the classroom, and the entire ideological apparatus of education, lay partly in what was coming to be seen as the proper physical segregation of children from adults' (1997: 12). School became a **space** for children.

Moreover, in Hendrick's view, in so far as school attendance was made compulsory for *all* children, school was important in establishing the idea of a national **childhood** that, on the surface, appeared to downplay differences of social class. No longer was it just the wealthy children who could be educated. However, it is here that the distinction between school and schooling becomes important, since it was not just the removal of children from the adult world of work into a separate space that is significant. What goes on when children attend school also matters.

Ostensibly, children go to school to be educated and, with the introduction in many countries of a national curriculum, the suggestion is that all children should receive the same education. However, what research on schooling shows is that first, children vary in the extent to which they benefit from schooling (in relation to grade attainment for example) and second, children learn many other things besides their intended educational lessons by attending school. Maden argues, for example, that for many children what increasing standardisation of levels of achievement has done is to make increased demands on children, and some children find it difficult to fit in with a school system which 'so stresses conformity and rigidity' (1999: 83). This is especially so if their home lives, and kinds of experiences they have outside school, differ sharply from the ethos and value systems perpetuated within it. Indeed, this may lead to some children being excluded from school. Often these are children who are disadvantaged because of their **ethnicity**, their special educational needs or because they have low self-esteem.

Connolly (2004) also shows how schooling can be experienced differently by children because of the ways in which it takes place. Through ethnographic work carried out in Northern Ireland, he shows how working-class boys are unable to fit into the schooling that is offered to them for three reasons: first, there is a mismatch between the kinds of authority children experience at home and at school, with the latter being experienced as more controlling; second, drawing on their parents' and other adults' experiences, many of whom are unemployed, the boys cannot see any advantage in education; and third, there is a 'fundamental mismatch between the dominant form of masculinity that some tend to subscribe to and the demands of the school', which are that boys be 'diligent, passive and hardworking' (2004: 217). The boys, on the other hand, place great importance on strength and physical prowess. All this, Connolly argues, makes the working-class boys' experiences of schooling very different from those of their middle-class counterparts, for whom there is a far closer match between the values and ethos at school and those they find at home. Meanwhile, Lewis (2003), in her study of elementary schools in California, examines the hidden and overt curriculum of the school to show how lessons about race and inequality are insinuated into children's lives at school.

It can be argued, therefore, that schooling is not just about education in terms of the imparting of knowledge; it is also about the production of children's conformity through the authority invested in adult teachers. In part this is because the school system can be viewed as an investment by the State in the preparation of children for their **future** as adult workers. Such a perspective contrasts strongly with the view espoused by educationalists, that the school is an institution designed to enable children's social and personal development. It should be noted, however, that the educational process will, of course, ultimately benefit the State by producing adults who can think creatively.

A rather different approach to schooling than the authoritarian and hierarchical experiences that many children have takes place within the Reggio Emilia pedagogy that has developed in Italy. Here children are positioned as co-constructors in the process of learning, rather than, as in more didactic educational systems, simply as the receivers of other people's (adults') knowledge. Within this system the school is 'a place that plays an active role in the children's search for meaning' rather than a place where children are taught (Rinaldi, 2005: 18).

Children's experiences of school depend therefore, in part, on the ethos of schooling that exists. In research carried out in northern England, for example, Christensen and James (2001) show that many 11-year-old children experience school as a treadmill of non-stop work that can, at times, feel rather boring. In part, this experience is a result of the temporal structure of the English school day and week, which means that children lack control over 'how and with whom they spend their time' (2001: 84). Lessons are organised and run by teachers who also have the authority, if they care to exercise it, to punish children by depriving them of their **play**-time – and this is the only time that is under children's control in the school day. Thus, while children appreciate the importance of getting a good education, they may not enjoy the experience of schooling through which that education is delivered.

Indeed, some have argued that attending school is a form of child **work** since, in learning their lessons, children are contributing to the future of the State (Qvortrup, 1995), and Field's (1995) study of children's experiences of the high-pressured Japanese school system confirms this. One aspect of schooling that children do appreciate, however, is play-time and as Blatchford (1998) has shown, for children this is a key aspect of their experiences of schooling. Play-time is when **friendship** flourishes and, for many children, going to school to meet their friends may be as important as, if not more important than, the education they will receive.

The receipt of education is considered to be a fundamental children's right, and there is a large body of educational research devoted to ensuring that good education is delivered to children appropriately. However, what research within **childhood studies** can contribute to this growing knowledge base is a more **child-focused** perspective that explores children's experiences of education as the process of schooling.

FURTHER READING

Blatchford, P. (1998) *Social Life in School*. London: Falmer.

Christensen, P. and James, A. (2001) 'What are schools for? The temporal experience of children's learning in Northern England', in L. Alanen and B. Mayall (eds), *Conceptualizing Child–Adult Relations*. London: Routledge/Falmer.

Connolly, P. (2004) *Boys and Schooling in the Early Years*. London: Routledge/Falmer.

Field, N. (1995) 'The child as labourer and consumer: The disappearance of childhood in contemporary Japan', in S. Stephens (ed.), *Children and the Politics of Culture*. Princeton, NJ: Princeton University Press.

Hendrick, H. (1997) *Children, Childhood and English Society 1800–1990*. Cambridge: Cambridge University Press.

Lewis, A. (2003) *Race in the Schoolyard: Negotiating the Color Line in Classrooms and Communities*. Camden, NJ: Rutgers University Press.

Maden, M. (1999) 'The challenge of children in the education system', in J. Tunstill (ed.), *Children and the State: Whose Problem?* London: Cassell.

Qvrotrup, J. (1995) 'From useful to useful: The historical continuity of children's constructive participation', in A. Ambert (ed.), *Sociological Studies of Children*, Vol. 7. Greenwich, CT: JAI Press.

Qvrotrup, J. and Kjørholt, A-T. (eds) (2011) *The Modern Child and the Flexible Labour Market: Early Childhood Education and Care*. Basingstoke: Palgrave Macmillan.

Rinaldi, C. (2005) 'Documentation and assessment: What is the relationship?' in P. Moss, A. Clark and A. Trine Kjørholt (eds), *Beyond Listening: Children's Perspectives on Early Childhood Services*. Bristol: The Policy Press.

Sexual Abuse

Sexual abuse includes a wide range of behaviours, all of which involve the encouragement or coercion of a child or young person to participate in sexual activities, whether or not they are aware of what is happening and whether or not such behaviour may be defined by others as abusive. Sexual abuse does not necessarily only involve physical contact (such as penetrative and non-penetrative sexual acts); it also includes activities that do not necessitate contact, such as involving children in the watching or production of pornography, watching the sexual activity of others, or encouraging children to behave in sexually inappropriate ways.

The (re-)emergence of child abuse as a social concern in the western world in the latter part of the 20th century initially focused on physical abuse – the so-called 'battered baby syndrome'. However, the focus of concern over the maltreatment of children has subsequently broadened to include emotional abuse, **neglect** and sexual abuse, although it is clear that child sexual abuse (CSA) may also be associated with any and all of these other forms of abuse.

Estimates of the extent of CSA vary but some researchers have suggested that, worldwide, 20 per cent of women and 5–10 per cent of men have experienced sexual abuse as children (Freyd et al., 2005). The extent and nature of CSA are intrinsically difficult to measure with any accuracy because it is probable that the large majority of such incidents remain undisclosed. It is clear, however, that CSA can be committed by members of a child's **family** as well as by adults who are not related to the child, that the majority of those who commit CSA do so against children who are known to them, and that, in the large majority of cases, it occurs in the home of the abuser or the victim.

CSA has both short- and long-term consequences for abused children. Moreover for some, although by no means all, it can lead to an increased risk that they will become abusers themselves. This phenomenon is referred to by some as 'the cycle of sexual abuse'. In the short term, children who are sexually abused may suffer physical injury or even death; on the other hand, there may be no physical effects whatever. They may also suffer a range of behavioural problems including anxiety, fear and aggression, as well as age-inappropriate sexual behaviour. It is debatable, however, whether a child will necessarily suffer any harm at all as a result of minor incidents, such as witnessing an offence of indecent exposure, even though this would constitute an act of CSA.

In the long term, for many children who have experienced sexual abuse, guilt and shame are invariably present, in addition to problems such as low self-esteem, lack of trust, anxiety and depression, self-harming behaviour and eating disorders. Such effects can have a major impact on a child's education and learning, as well as on their interpersonal relationships, both in childhood and often well into adulthood (for more detail, see, for example, Hanks and Stratton, 2007). The consequences of being sexually abused as a child can be severe, although it is clear that not every child who is abused in this way will necessarily suffer seriously from all or even any of these effects.

The extent to which children do suffer such consequences will be determined by several factors, including the nature and extent of the abuse, the child's relationship with their abuser, the period of time over which a child is exposed to the abuse, and its frequency. In addition, the **resilience** of the child, as well as the cultural context and the reactions of others, are important variables. It is also arguable that the 'moral panic' that has surrounded child abuse, and particularly CSA, in recent years in western industrialised countries has had a significant impact on adult reactions to disclosures of sexual abuse, which can in turn amplify the impact of the experience on a child.

In other countries and cultural contexts, such as Thailand for example, CSA in the form of child prostitution is a more common response to **poverty** (Montgomery, 2001), and in such a social and economic context what would be regarded in the West as CSA is a way in which children can **work** to provide much-needed economic support for their parents and families. Child prostitution is thus supported, and sometimes encouraged, by parents. Although those children involved may rightly be regarded as victims of poverty, for many their prostitution is a valued, legitimate and socially accepted or necessary means of contributing to their families' economic survival, and therefore not something that will necessarily result in the kinds of consequences described above.

Nonetheless, adults' concern about CSA in many countries locates the issue firmly in the context of the child **protection**/child **welfare** debate and the **rights** of children to be protected under Article 3 and, in particular, Article 34 of the UNCRC, which requires States 'to protect the child from all forms of sexual exploitation and sexual abuse'.

The nature of the debate about CSA, however, often means that, as with many other aspects of their lives, children's perspectives on such issues are not valued or heard. Thus their **agency** and the decisions/choices they make (decisions which are, of course, subject to various constraints, just as they are for adults) are almost always ignored or dismissed because of the symbolic importance of issues such as CSA to the child-saving agenda of adults. As Montgomery observes, for the children she studied in Thailand

> selling sex is an accepted part of their lives, and while no child says that sex in this way is pleasurable for them, it is still seen as an easy way to earn money ... for the children themselves, it is often viewed as yet another hazard to be negotiated in a life full of difficulties and poverty. (2001: 98–9)

This is not to deny for a moment that many children can and do suffer grievously at the hands of adults as a result of CSA and that they deserve and have the right to protection; it is to acknowledge, however, that there is no single cultural frame or set of mores that can be applied to all sexual relationships between adults and children. Not least this is because of the centrality of the issues of **age** and biological development in the **social construction** of childhood and, in particular, childhood **innocence**. This dilemma is perhaps highlighted by considering the question of the age of consent (the age at which a child can consent to have sexual relationships with another person) and as a result of which sexual behaviour may therefore not be defined as CSA. Historically, in many societies this has been 12–14, but now only about half of European countries do not criminalise consensual sexual relations between 14-year-olds, and in the large majority of countries the minimum age of consent is 16. Importantly, what such legal restrictions fail to take account of, once again, is the **agency** of children and young people in relation to their own sexual behaviour, their reasonable expectations of autonomy in relation to this, and the power of adolescent sexuality in influencing this.

Related to this is the age at which a child or young person can marry, although this may not necessarily be the same as the age of consent. Historically, this has been as young as 7 and sometimes even younger, although the age for consummation of such marriages was often the same as the age of consent for sexual activity (i.e. 12). In the Ancient Greek world, it was common for men as old as 30 to marry pubescent girls; and in Rome, the average age for girls to marry was 14. Such practices should be considered alongside the current legal position today where in many western countries, consensual sexual intercourse between a 15-year-old girl and a 16-year-old boy would be illegal.

Such issues highlight the complexity of sexual relations with, and between, children and young people. They also underline the importance of avoiding absolutist assumptions about what constitutes CSA, the need to understand different historical and cultural contexts and, above all, the importance of acknowledging and taking account of the views of children and young people, and recognising the extent of their agency in such matters. What precisely constitutes child sexual abuse and its regulation is, as much as childhood itself, a matter of children's experience, as well as its social, cultural and legal construction.

FURTHER READING

Barrett, D. (2002) *Knowledge of Evil: Child Prostitution and Child Sexual Abuse in Twentieth Century England*. Devon: Willan.

Freyd, J., Putnam, F. and Lyon, T. (2005) 'The science of child sexual abuse', *Science*, 308: 501.

Graupner, H. and Bullough, V. (eds) (2004) *Adolescence, Sexuality and the Criminal Law: Multi-disciplinary Perspectives*. Birmingham: Haworth.

Hanks, H. and Stratton, P. (2007) 'Common forms and consequences of child abuse', in K. Wilson and A. James (eds), *The Child Protection Handbook: The Practitoner's Guide to Safeguarding Children* (3rd edn). Edinburgh: Ballière Tindall/Elsevier.

Montgomery, H. (2001) *Modern Babylon? Prostituting Children in Thailand*. London: Berghahn.

O'Connell Davidson, J. (2005) *Children in the Global Sex Trade*. Cambridge: Polity.

Pearce, J. (2006) 'Who needs to be involved in safeguarding sexually exploited young people?', *Child Abuse Review*, 15: 326–40.

Wilson, K. and James, A.L. (eds) (2007) *The Child Protection Handbook: The Practitioner's Guide to Safeguarding Children* (3rd edn). Edinburgh: Ballière Tindall/Elsevier.

Sexualisation

The material cultural practices of treating young girls as if they were adult women.

The sexualisation of children is a misnomer since, on the whole, this process refers much more to girls than to boys. It is a concern that has arisen out of the growing recognition of **children as consumers** and marketeers' targeting of scaled-down versions of adult clothing, such as push-up bras and thongs, at pre-teen girl children.

Concern also focuses on the ways in which young girls and teenagers are being drawn into the 'beauty industry' by the marketing of a range of beauty products directly to them. Such practices, it is argued, focus undue attention on the body and its potential for sex appeal at an inappropriate **age**. These anxieties about the sexualisation of children extend also to children's exposure to different kinds of media. Here it is suggested that children might be harmed by being able to access **age**-inappropriate material such as sexually explicit films, and they are, therefore, in need of **protection** from it.

Such moral concerns are, however, not new. As Holland argues, 'the eroticization of young girls has had a long history, with the sexual **innocence** of the young girl serving to make her the most perfect object of men's desires, the inexperienced woman' (1992: 127). Indeed, the assumption about the child's lack of sexual awareness forms a symbolic conceptual divide between adults and children, even though the **age** at which children are permitted to indulge in sexual activity varies between cultures. Buckingham (2011) argues, therefore, that the concern about sexualisation arises from anxieties, on the one hand, about the loss of childish **innocence** and, on the other hand, the fear that such premature expression of sexuality might increase children's risk to sexual predation and **abuse** by adults. It is also believed that the sexualisation of children will encourage them to experiment with sex far earlier than they might otherwise.

These concerns, however, assume a rather simplistic 'cause and effect' model: that is, early exposure to sexual content/knowledge/images necessarily leads to a greater and promiscuous interest in sex. However, as Buckingham and Bragg's (2004) research into young people, sex and the **media** showed, while older children may learn things about sex from the media this does not inevitably encourage them to adopt more sexualised behaviour. Younger children may, in any case, not understand the sexual messages they encounter and tend to ignore them. Indeed, research in Norway with 10-year-old girls found that even though they were interested in fashion, they did not associate eroticism with the wearing of cool, fashionable clothes; for them, 'the issue of sexuality … was something "yucky" and embarassing' (Rysst, 2010: 240). As Rysst argues, therefore, 10-year-old girls (and boys) do not share adult understandings of sexuality because they have not had the same sexual bodily experiences. The girls also did not know the meaning of the term 'sexy', seeing it simply as something to do with looking nice and wearing fashionable clothes. While understanding that this, in turn, might make them seem attractive to boys, the girls considered themselves too young to engage in such behaviour. Rysst warns, therefore, against assuming that adults and children interpret bodily representations in the same manner.

The issues surrounding the sexualisation of children are highlighted poignantly in debates about the moral impropriety (or otherwise) of the child beauty pageants held in many parts of the world, where considerable cash prizes are at stake. In considering their impact, Giroux (1998) examines the case of the murder of 6-year-old JonBenét Ramsey in the USA, who was encouraged by her parents to take part in child beauty pageants that were screened on national television. As a contestant she wore tight, revealing clothing and red lipstick to

sexualisation

accompany her bleached blond hair. As Giroux observes, the mass popular screening of this beauty pageant 'belied the assumption that the voyeuristic fascination with the sexualized child was confined to the margins of society – inhabited by freaks and psychopaths' (1998: 270). Indeed, in Giroux's view, beauty pageants epitomise the contradictions present in modern consumer culture that involve the commodification of the female body alongside an insistence on childhood **innocence**: 'practices that might be seen in other contexts as abusive to children are defined within the beauty pageant culture as good, clean, family entertainment' (1998: 276).

O'Connell Davidson (2005) also investigates the ways in which the boundaries between childhood and adulthood are blurred by the phenomenon of children who are involved in the **global** sex trade. Structural factors, such as sex tourism and trafficking, together with the symbolic **sexualisation** of childhood **innocence** in pornography, work to sustain this industry and forms of **child sexual abuse**.

FURTHER READING

Buckingham, D. (2011) *The Material Child: Growing up in Consumer Culture*. Cambridge: Polity.
Buckingham, D. and Bragg, S. (2004) *Young People, Sex and the Media: The 'facts of life'?* London: Palgrave.
Giroux, H.A. (1998) 'Stealing innocence', in H. Jenkins (ed.), *The Children's Culture Reader*. New York: New York University Press.
Holland, P. (1992) *What is a Child?* London: Virago.
O'Connell Davidson, J. (2005) *Children in the Global Sex Trade*. Cambridge: Polity.
Rysst, M. (2010) '"Hello – We're only in the fifth grade!!": Children's rights, inter-generationality and constructions of gender in public discourses about childhood', in D. Buckingham and V. Tingstad (eds), *Childhood and Consumer Culture*. Basingstoke: Palgrave Macmillan.

Social Actor

A concept that recognises the active part that children can play in everyday social life.

The idea that children should be regarded as social actors received its first strong statement in social science writing during the 1970s. In an anthropological study of children in English playgrounds, Hardman argued that 'children should be seen as people to be studied in their own right and not just as receptacles of adult teaching' and that through doing so, researchers would gain rather different perspectives – child perspectives – on the social world (1973: 85). In Hardman's view, earlier research, mainly from within developmental psychology, had failed to acknowledge children as people who might be studied as social actors because the overarching concern was to document children's physiological and psychological development. This focus, she argued, 'muted' **children's voices** in society; children's views were neither sought nor given much significance, since their role in society was simply conceived of in terms of their **futurity**. They were in an apprenticeship for adult life.

At the same time, in the USA, Bluebond-Langner's (1978) pioneering work with child cancer patients revealed the extent of children's **agency** once they were regarded as having an active part to play in society. Drawing on symbolic interactionists such as Denzin (1973), Bluebond-Langner argued that children possess a sense of self that allows them to 'interpret the behaviour of others and act on the basis on their own interpretations' (1978: 7). Through participant observation, she detailed the ways in which children adopted different kinds of behaviours towards different people in different settings, revealing that 'children can move from one social world to another and act appropriately in each world' (1978: 12).

Out of these early studies, therefore, has emerged one of the central tenets within childhood studies: 'that children must be seen as active in the construction and determination of their own social lives, the lives of those around them and of the societies in which they live' (Prout and James, 1990: 8). No longer can they be seen as 'just the passive subjects of social structure or processes' (1990: 8).

Although now accepted as a key paradigm shift in **research with children**, this initial conceptualisation of children as social actors has been subjected to a number of refinements. Mayall (2002), for example, has argued that children should be seen as agents, rather than just actors. This subtle distinction draws attention to the effects that children's actions can have. As Mayall says, they can make a difference 'to a relationship, to a decision, to the workings of a set of social assumptions or constraints' (2002: 21). This focus on agency is core to the **cultural politics of childhood** since it assigns children a degree of power to effect social change.

For Lee (2001), on the other hand, the concept of agency is troubling, since it attributes to children the same kinds of independence that adults have; this, he argues, denies the facts of children's biological, physiological and psychological immaturity. In his view, the notion of actor is preferable as long as it is not understood to imply that children are complete, rounded individuals who are able to act totally independently. Using the insights from actor-network theory, Lee argues for a modified conceptualisation of children as social actors. Rather than positioning children as independent social actors as a starting point for researching children's lives, Lee argues that we have to explore, empirically, *how* children are enabled *to be* social actors. To do this we have to see them, he argues, as located in a network of interdependencies of different kinds, in the context of particular sets of circumstances. These will have an impact upon the ways in which they can act.

While this would appear at first sight to open up a rather different ontological status for children – and one which, in Lee's work, lays stress on their immaturity – this is not the case. The symbolic interactionist legacy upon which more conventional formulations of children as social actors is built, which depicts human capacity for self-reflection, interpretation and independent thought, does not place the individual outside of 'the social'. Indeed, interdependencies and connections with others are *precisely* the kinds of relationships through which all human social action unfolds. In regard to children, the difference lies in the degree to which children are *permitted* to act independently by those around them, particularly adults. It is this that may limit their experience of being independent actors, and thereby have an effect upon what they choose to do, but this does not nullify the argument that all children have the capacity to be reflexive social actors.

FURTHER READING

Bluebond-Langner, M. (1978) *The Private Worlds of Dying Children*. Princeton, NJ: Princeton University Press.

Denzin, N. (1973) *Children and their Caretakers*. New Brunswick, NJ: Transaction Books.

Hardman, C. (1973) 'Can there be an anthropology of children?', *Journal of the Anthropological Society of Oxford*, 4(1): 85–99.

Lee, N. (2001) *Childhood and Society*. Buckingham: Open University Press.

Mayall, B. (2002) *Towards a Sociology of Childhood: Thinking from Children's Lives*. Buckingham: Open University Press.

Prout, A. and James, A. (1990) 'A new paradigm for the sociology of childhood? Provenance, promise and problems', in A. James and A. Prout (eds), *Constructing and Reconstructing Childhood*. Basingstoke: Falmer.

Social Construction

A theoretical perspective that explores the ways in which 'reality' is negotiated in everyday life through people's interactions and through sets of discourses.

The suggestion that 'reality' is socially constructed has its roots in the symbolic-interactionist paradigm, which explores the ways in which individuals are involved in the ongoing 'making' of everyday life through their actions. However, it was the sociologists Peter Berger and Thomas Luckman who developed the concept of the social construction of reality in their book of that title, which first appeared in 1967. This argued that the taken-for-granted 'reality' of everyday life arises through the interactions people have with one another and with the environments in which they live, including both the cultural and natural, material world. This process accounts not only for the different 'realities' which people in different parts of the world experience, but also for the differences within any one society that arise, for example, through people's differential access to wealth. It is in this sense, then, that sociological theory argues that 'reality' is socially constructed.

The importance of this theoretical perspective for the development of **childhood studies** has been immense. First, it was core to the early discussions that took place about the nature of **childhood** which led to the question being raised about the extent to which childhood is a natural or a social phenomenon. While clearly

key concepts in childhood studies

the concept of childhood refers, in general terms, to the early part of the human life-course, the ways in which this period of growth and development is understood vary in different cultures. This is evident in the various ways in which children are treated and the different expectations that are held about their capabilities and **competence**. The example of **working children** brings this into sharp perspective, with some children in countries in the majority South being thought capable, for example, of taking on adult-type work activities, while the activities that children in the industrialised countries of the North are allowed to engage in are being increasingly restricted because children are thought to be especially **vulnerable** to harm and risk. It is in this sense, then, that childhood can be said to be socially constructed. Indeed, that ideas of childhood are negotiated in this way, through the everyday interactions of people in society, is what makes the globalisation of a unitary idea of childhood, through the United Nations Convention on the Rights of the Child (**UNCRC**) 1989, problematic to implement.

Social constructionism is also important for understanding how the ideas about children and childhood that are to be found in the **representations** and discourses of different societies impact on children's everyday lives and experiences. Core to the **cultural politics of childhood** (James and James, 2004), ideas about what children are like, the kinds of activities they are capable of undertaking, the kinds of **needs** they have, the risks they face and what is in their **best interests** come to be expressed in the laws and policies that are drawn up by governments to regulate the lives of children. In this way, then, the 'reality' that children experience as everyday life (e.g. the law that says they must go to school) has been constructed not only through parents' and teachers' interactions with children and their recognition that laws have to be obeyed, but also through the ideas embedded in that law that the **schooling** of children is an important investment for the future of the nation.

FURTHER READING

Berger, P. and Luckman, T. (1967) *The Social Construction of Reality*. Garden City, NY: Anchor.
James, A. and James, A.L. (2004) *Constructing Childhood: Theory, Policy and Social Practice*. Basingstoke: Palgrave Macmillan.
Jenks, C. (1996) *Childhood*. London: Routledge.
Wyness, M. (2006) *Childhood and Society: An Introduction to the Sociology of Childhood*. Basingstoke: Palgrave.

social world

Social World

117

The context of children's everyday lives as a social group of children and in relation to the adult world.

One of the first people to suggest that children might be regarded as having their own separate culture or social world was the social anthropologist Charlotte Hardman. In her ethnographic study of English children's school playground games, she drew on the work of the folklorists Iona and Peter Opie who had, over many years, put together collections of children's **play**, games, songs and other oral lore. These volumes, published in 1959 and 1969, revealed the existence of many children's games and rhymes that not only had endured across the centuries, but were also to be found in a variety of different forms in different parts of the UK. The Opies argued that, due to their persistence across time and space, these rhymes and games represented a separate children's culture, 'unnoticed by the sophisticated world', and one that exists among children in **spaces** usually outside the home and away from adults (1959: 2).

In her own anthropological work, Hardman developed this idea and suggested that this culture should be seen as representing a children's social world, one that has its own internal order and sets of rules and that is semi-autonomous from the wider adult world. She cited examples of the ways in which children, through the games they play, designate different areas of the playground with special names and characterise some places as having magical properties. Children share this knowledge with one another and abide by these special cultural rules. That adults rarely take much notice of children's own social worlds led Hardman to conclude that children could be regarded as a 'muted group' in society, in the sense that their views and perspectives on the world are silenced by the dominant adult world and often remain elusive to adult researchers. Hardman argued, therefore, that in order for **children's voices** to be heard, they should be regarded as 'people to be studied in their own right and not just as receptacles of adult teaching', as happens more traditionally in work on **developmental psychology** and **socialisation** (1973: 87). Moreover, she suggested that children – not adults – should be the **competent** informants about this world. It was this recognition of the importance of children's own social worlds that was fundamental to the development of the emergent paradigm in the new social studies of childhood that appeared in the 1990s.

A number of classic studies have explored the alternative social worlds of children. Corsaro's (1979) study of **friendship** practices among small children describes the ritualised patterns of behaviour through which small children initiate contact with their peers. The access rituals used by 4-year-old children to gain entry into **play** activities represent, for Corsaro, an illustration of 'the organisation of the child's world on its own terms' (1979: 317). Andrew Pollard (1985) explored the sub-groups that existed in the peer relations of a group of primary school children in England. His description vividly reveals a separate world of children, one in which conformity (or not) to the authority structures of the adult world confers particular kinds of identities on certain groups of children. Meanwhile, James's (1993) study demonstrated how children's identities were structured by the demands of the peer and friendship groups to which they belonged. Such studies therefore confirm Hardman's suggestion that 'there is in childhood a self-regulating, autonomous world which does not necessarily reflect early development of adult culture' (1973: 87).

However, while such studies are important in revealing, for the first time, an autonomous child's social world, through the eyes and voices of children themselves, criticism has centred on the extent to which researchers have over-emphasised the separation between children's and adults' culture. It is suggested that attention must be given not only to the autonomy of children's worlds but also to the ways in which these are necessarily situated within, and therefore potentially shaped by, the dominant adult culture, if only through the role of different **generations** in the transmission of knowledge about childhood experiences.

Corsaro, for example, tackles this problem through the concept of **interpretive reproduction**. He uses this to capture the ways in which 'children create and participate in their own unique peer cultures by creatively taking or appropriating information from the adult world to address their own peer concerns' (1997: 18). In bridging the supposed gulf between children's and adults' worlds, this concept also helps explain how **socialisation** takes place between children in the context of the **peer group**, which is the central feature of children's social worlds. More recently other work (Spilsbury and Korbin, 2004) has begun to explore the concept of social capital in relation to children's experiences of neighbourhood life in the USA, investigating the ways and extent to which the social worlds of children intersect with, or come into conflict with, those of the adults whose **space** they share (see also Morrow, 2001).

The concept of a social world brings into sharp focus some key issues in **childhood studies**: how to acknowledge and give weight to children's own social worlds and perspectives while, at the same time, also recognising that children live much of their lives in the company of adults and, indeed, within a world largely defined for them by adults.

FURTHER READING

Corsaro, W. (1979) '"We're friends, right?": Children's use of access rituals in a nursery school', *Language in Society*, 8: 315–36.

Corsaro, W. (1997) *The Sociology of Childhood*. London: Pine Forge Press.

Hardman, C. (1973) 'Can there be an anthropology of children?', *Journal of the Anthropological Society of Oxford*, 4(1): 85–99.

James, A. (1993) *Childhood Identities*. Edinburgh: Edinburgh University Press.

Morrow, V. (2001) *Networks and Neighbourhoods: Children's and Young People's Perspectives*. Report for the Health Development Agency Social Capital for Health series. London: Health Development Agency.

Opie, I. and Opie, P. (1959) *The Lore and Language of School Children*. London: Paladin.

Opie, I. and Opie, P. (1969) *Children's Games in Street and Playground*. Oxford: Oxford University Press.

Pollard, A. (1985) *The Social World of the Primary School*. London: Holt, Rinehart & Winston.

Spilsbury, J.C. and Korbin, J.E. (2004) 'Negotiating the dance: Social capital from the perspective of the neighbourhood, children and adults', in P.B. Pufall and R.P. Unsworth (eds), *Rethinking Childhood*. New Brunswick, NJ: Rutgers University Press.

Socialisation

> *The process whereby children are taught, and learn, to meet the expectations of, and to fit into, a given society.*

The concept of socialisation has a long and varied history within the social sciences but, at its most simplistic level, it can be understood as the process through which children are 'taught' the social mores pertinent to any particular society or culture. This teaching is both explicit and implicit, both intentional and unintentional. Traditionally regarded as something that is 'done' to children, more recently socialisation is being explored in terms of the ways in which children acquire the social attributes pertinent to 'being human' in any particular society. Although most often used in relation to children, it is nonetheless a process which continues throughout life as people move in and between different societies, or have to get to know the roles and expectations that accompany new stages in the life-course, or as they move into new social institutions.

It was in the 1950s, in the work of the sociologist Talcott Parsons (1951), that the foundations of the concept of socialisation were first articulated, when he set out his vision of the ways in which society functions. For Parsons, the socialisation of children was fundamental to the future functioning of the social system since, he argued, it is during childhood that a society's value orientations are laid down. For society to endure, according to Parsons, its citizens had not only to conform to a common set of social rules but also to have a consensual view of the world; without these, 'society' simply would not be possible. Thus Parsons sought to explain how this consensus develops and, for him, the answer lay in the existence of sets of social norms and rules that constrain the actions of individuals and bind them together. Through identification with these social norms, individuals become committed to the social system and thereby help sustain its functioning.

The big question, though, is how is such a commitment engendered? For Parsons, the answer can be found in the role the **family** plays in giving the **child** particular role models and values to identify with. In this way, the family becomes the bedrock of the social system through ensuring the primary socialisation of the child. Indeed, within the Parsonian account, children, as unsocialised beings, represented a threat to society's continued functioning; it was the family's job initially to ensure that children internalised the appropriate norms and values.

Later critiques of the Parsonian model argued that what it produces is an overly socialised conception of human life (Wrong, 1961), one that suggests that individuals are entirely moulded by the values and social norms of the societies in which they live. Further, it is a view of the child that presupposes such an inherent plasticity and passivity that it would seem to be fundamentally different from adults, which begs the question of how it is possible that children do eventually grow up. But most of all, the Parsonian model of socialisation can be criticised for its lack of attention to process. While it might offer an explanation of what happens during the social reproduction of society, it is not able to explain how exactly this takes place, nor what part children have to play in it. Through drawing extensively on the language of psychology, sociology mystified rather than clarified this process. Writing in 1960, Elkin describes socialisation in the following manner: 'the socialising agents teach, serve as models and invite participation. Through their ability to offer gratification and deprivations they induce cooperation and learning and prevent disrupting deviance' (1960: 101). Such a deterministic account of the ways in which children become integrated into society left little room for any account of children's **agency** in that process.

In later work, however, closer attention has been paid to the processes through which socialisation takes place, by exploring not only the ways in which children are 'taught' but also how and what they learn, both implicitly and explicitly. Significantly, this has involved seeing children as **social actors** who engage with the **social world**, rather than just as the passive receivers of adult wisdom as in the Parsonian model. Thus, for example, in Briggs's (1998) account of Inuit child-rearing, there are detailed descriptions of how children learn the moral values necessary to an Inuit way of life. This occurs through the teasing games (games that repeatedly threaten or challenge children) that adults play with children, and it is through their active **participation** in these often dangerous and emotionally charged games that Inuit children come to understand the core values of being an Inuit.

Socialisation is, however, not solely a process that takes place from adult to child and, in his classic study of children's **friendships** and **peer groups**, Corsaro (1985) shows the ways in which children socialise one another into the rules and social norms that define children's own social worlds and, through the process of **interpretive reproduction**, also come to understand the wider world of adults to which they belong and in which they must learn how to act.

FURTHER READING

Briggs, J. (1998) *Inuit Morality Play*. New Haven, CT: Yale University Press.
Corsaro, W.A. (1985) *Friendship and Peer Culture in the Early Years*. Norwood, NJ: Ablex.
Elkin, F. (1960) *The Child and Society: The Process of Socialisation*. New York: Random House.
Parsons, T. (1951) *The Social System*. London: Routledge & Kegan Paul.
Wrong, D. (1961) 'The oversocialized conception of man in modern sociology', *American Sociological Review*, 26: 184–93.

Spaces for Children and Children's Places

The idea that certain physical spaces are conceptualised as being specifically suitable for use by children; it also describes the spaces which children themselves choose to occupy and make use of in their everyday lives and the ways in which they understand the environments that they inhabit.

Research into children's spaces has been undertaken from within a wide variety of disciplines, with the main contributions coming from sociology, anthropology, geography and psychology. While there is some overlap between these approaches, in terms of the ways in which each discipline addresses the conceptual relationship between children and space, there are also some significant differences. For example, while developmental psychologists might be interested in the impact that the physical environment has on young children's physical and cognitive development and well-being, geographers and sociologists are often more interested in understanding the meanings that children attribute to particular spaces and the ways in which they choose to use them, as Hart's early (1979) work on children's use of space in the USA demonstrates.

One widespread assumption is that children have an affinity with the natural world that is somehow inherent to their being children, and often this is used by policymakers and planners to draw attention to the benefits for **health** and well-being that supposedly accrue to children through their contact with nature. Reviewing a range of experimental and correlational studies, Taylor and Juo (2006) are hard put, however, to find much conclusive evidence to support this assumption. While tentatively concluding that 'contact with nature is supportive of healthy child development', they caution that any causal relationship is not yet proven (2006: 136). It may be, for example, that it is the *kinds* of activities that children are able to do in outdoor green spaces, as opposed to indoor spaces, that are facilitative of healthy development, rather than the contact with the natural world per se. The Norwegian Nature Kindergarten movement, which has developed in recent years, provides a good example here, as do the Forest Schools now appearing elsewhere in Europe. Nielsen (2008), for instance, describes how in the outdoor kindergartens that have been established for pre-school children in Norwegian forests and woodland, 3- and 4-year-old children spend their days, even in extremely cold weather, learning skills of nature-craft that teach self-reliance and independence. For Nielsen, however, this is not just – or even – a matter of health; it is about teaching children what it is to be a 'proper' Norwegian: that is, someone with a love of nature and the outdoor life.

Other research (Holloway and Valentine, 2000) has explored how discourses of the rural idyll shape other adult attitudes towards children in industrialised societies, where parents regard the countryside as somehow a safer and better place for children to grow up. However, as Matthews and Tucker (2006) note, when rural teenagers themselves talk about life in rural areas, their accounts tend to stress its negative aspects. They describe being bored and see themselves as having a restricted social life due to their lack of independent mobility, given the poor transport services that often characterise the rural hinterlands of urban industrial societies.

These studies exploring the benefits and drawbacks of rural idylls speak, for the most part, to children who live in modern industrialised societies. For children of the majority South, who live and **work** in poor rural areas, their contact with nature is much more mundane, since the natural world provides them with a living. For **working children** and their families, it is the urban centres that may appear to promise a better life.

As these examples indicate, there is a close relationship between the concepts of space and place. Place is more than simply a geographical location: it is a space imbued with social and cultural meanings. Thus, in their discussion of children and their environments, Spencer and Blades (2006) make an important distinction between environments *for* children and environments *of* children. Through this, they draw attention to the fact that some places are designed specifically for children, to meet their **needs** (these are *for* children), whereas other spaces (*of* children) are left-over kinds of spaces in the environment that children appropriate for their own use. Thus, for example, **schools** are institutional spaces, intended for the schooling of children, whereas waste-ground and urban streets are often used by children for **play**.

What is important about this distinction is that it draws attention to the ways in which meaning is attributed to space (Fog Olwig and Gulløv, 2003). For example, spaces that have been designed and designated *for* children may be considered to be **child-friendly**: that is to say, they are said to meet the needs and interests that children have. However, the extent of children's **participation** in the design and function of that space is often limited. This means that these places may represent adults' views of the kinds of places that they think are suitable for children – often safe, protected places, like playgrounds, that are separated from other spaces and often controlled by adults. Children themselves may, however, find these spaces too restricting, preferring to create their own places on their own terms. Matthews et al. (2000) show, for example, how children and young people use the street as an important place for socialising and that this re-use of the street is as important for girls as it is for boys.

A relatively new space for children is 'cyberspace', and as Valentine et al. (2000) argue, children's facility with new technology is giving them alternative ways to communicate with their friends and to develop their hobbies on-line. While adult concern often focuses on information and communications technology (ICT) as damaging to children's **welfare** and well-being, fostering social isolation through encouraging them to stay indoors rather than go outside to play, much **child-focused research** demonstrates that cyberspace is not, in fact, isolating children from their friends: indeed, it may be helping to foster wider **friendships**. Children's access to and participation in cyberspace also raise adult fears about children's **vulnerability** and **innocence**, and therefore their need for **protection**. However, while there are examples of children accessing pornographic websites and being 'groomed' by older people through chat rooms, Valentine et al. show that 'children tend to use ICT in balanced and sophisticated ways' that are not, in general, harmful (2000: 170).

Research on space and place within childhood studies draws attention then to the importance of **structure** in the sequestration of places designed to separate children from adults. However, it also enables exploration of children's **agency** in the many studies of the innovative ways in which children take over or appropriate different spaces for a range of activities and, in so doing, transform these into children's places (Rasmussen, 2004)

spaces for children and children's places

123

FURTHER READING

Fog Olwig, K. and Gulløv, E. (eds) (2003) *Children's Places: Cross-cultural Perspectives*. London: Routledge.

Hart, R. (1979) *Children's Experiences of Place*. New York: Irvington.

Holloway, S.L. and Valentine, G. (eds) (2000) *Children's Geographies: Playing, Living and Learning.* London: Routledge.

Matthews, H. and Tucker, F. (2006) 'On the other side of the tracks: The pyschogeographies and everyday lives of rural teenagers in the UK', in C. Spencer and M. Blades (eds), *Children and their Environments.* Cambridge: Cambridge University Press.

Matthews, H., Limb, M. and Taylor, M. (2000) 'The street as third space', in S.L. Holloway and G. Valentine (eds), *Children's Geographies: Playing, Living and Learning.* London: Routledge.

Nielsen, R.D. (2008) 'Children in nature: Cultural ideas and social practices in Norway', in A. James and A.L. James (eds), *European Childhoods: Cultures, Politics and Childhoods in Europe.* Basingstoke: Palgrave Macmillan.

Rasmussen, K. (2004) 'Places for children – children's places', *Childhood,* 11(2): 155–73.

Spencer, C. and Blades, M. (2006) 'An introduction', in C. Spencer and M. Blades (eds), *Children and Their Environments.* Cambridge: Cambridge University Press.

Taylor, A.F. and Juo, F.E. (2006) 'Is contact with nature important for healthy child development? State of the evidence', in C. Spencer and M. Blades (eds), *Children and their Environments.* Cambridge: Cambridge University Press.

Valentine, G., Holloway, S.L. and Bingham, N. (2000) 'Transforming cyberspace: Children's interventions in the new public sphere', in S.L. Holloway and G. Valentine (eds), *Children's Geographies: Playing, Living and Learning.* London: Routledge.

Standpoint

> *The structural context within which children's experiences and perspectives should be understood as shaped by power relations.*

Standpoint theory, as used within **childhood studies**, has its roots in the feminist critique of sociology. This argued that many sociological concepts and theories had been developed from the point of view of men and that, because of this, women's experiences of the world have often been undervalued or misrepresented. This led to the politicisation of women's experiences and enabled women to challenge the status quo of masculine power within the social order. For some sociologists of childhood, therefore, the lessons of standpoint theory offer a useful way to reposition children within the social order by acknowledging their subordinate position vis-à-vis adults, to be understood in terms of **generation**. Mayall argues, for example, that 'just as gender emerged as a crucial concept for analysing relationships between the sexes, so generation is coming to be seen as key to understanding child–adult relationships' (2002: 25).

Accordingly, children can be seen as belonging to a **minority group**, a status that is underpinned by a whole range of social, political and economic inequalities that separate children from adults. In this structural sense, **childhood** represents a shared experience that is common to all children. Core to this experience are the power relations that enable adults to maintain control over children, forcing them into positions of subordination and dependency. To explore the world from the standpoint of children entails acknowledging the importance that this generational position has for shaping children's everyday experiences and understandings of the social relationships in which they are involved. Thus, for example, Mayall (2002) shows in her study of children living in London, England, that the children she interviewed valued childhood positively, and enjoyed some of the freedom and fun that mark out a modern western childhood. Nonetheless, they also recognised their subordinate position as children and felt constrained by the lack of opportunities they had to participate in decision making. They also commented on the lack of respect adults often showed to them. As Mayall observes, children's accounts 'encompass understandings of their social status, and its relation to the social status of adulthood' (2002: 136). Adopting a child standpoint is important for sociologists such as Mayall because, through doing so, it becomes possible to see how children are positioned in society, how their lives are shaped by adults, and how children themselves might work towards reshaping the social order and children's position within it. In this sense, adopting a child standpoint becomes a 'political enterprise' (2002: 139).

However, acknowledging that children's lives and experiences are shaped by the **structure** of the contexts within which children live out their lives suggests that, alongside children's generational position, account has also to be given of the ways in which class, **gender** and **ethnicity** impact upon children's everyday lives. For some sociologists this means that attention must be paid to childhood **diversity** and to the differences in children's experiences, despite their common status. James et al. point out, for example, that 'being a child of a prosperous middle-class urban family in Rio is not the same as being a child of a poor share-cropping family in north-east Brazil' (1998: 130). It is arguable, therefore, that the generational order is not the most important structural factor shaping children's experiences and a child standpoint. Moreover, what children themselves accomplish as **social actors/agents** in shaping the course of their everyday lives may also contribute to the ways in which childhood is experienced (James and James, 2004).

The debate about standpoint theory hinges ultimately on the ways in which the relationship between structure and agency is understood by theorists and where they place most emphasis in their accounts of childhood. Qvortrup (1994), for example, argues strongly that it is important to focus on the commonalities that unite children as a generational category in order that the impact of the broader sweep of social forces upon the status of childhood can be examined. Without this, he argues, it becomes impossible for children to benefit from childhood research that has a child's standpoint at its core. Others argue that such universalising of children's experiences ignores not only the individuality of children but also their capacities as social actors (e.g. James and James, 2004).

standpoint

FURTHER READING

James, A. and James, A.L. (2004) *Constructing Childhood: Theory, Policy and Social Practice.* Basingstoke: Palgrave Macmillan.

James, A., Jenks, C. and Prout, A. (1998) *Theorizing Childhood.* Cambridge: Polity.

Mayall, B. (2002) *Towards a Sociology of Childhood.* Buckingham: Open University Press.

Qvortrup, J. (1994) 'Childhood matters: An introduction', in J. Qvortrup, M. Bardy, G. Sgritta and H. Wintersberger (eds), *Childhood Matters.* Aldershot: Avebury.

Street Children

> *Children who live and/or **work** on the street.*

While the definition above suffices as an introduction to this concept, it is also in some ways misleading, since defining street children is intimately linked to the different ways in which such children are conceptualised. And as Gigengack (2008) argues, these conceptualisations vary in relation to the ways in which such children are 'problematised' – as either a 'problem' to be dealt with by the State or as a 'cause' to be taken up by NGOs and other activists seeking to help those children who live and **work** on the street. These different **representations** are revealing, he suggests, of the implicit transgressive comparison with 'normal' childhood that the phenomenon of street children engenders.

In an early formulation of this problem, Glauser (1997) argues, for example, for the need to distinguish between the different ways in which children engage with the street. For some, a life on the street may mean that they live there permanently, in social groups with other children, having broken all contact with their **family**. Others, however, may simply be working on the street (selling or begging) and then return home to their families at night. In this sense, they may simply be part of the many millions of children in the majority South who have to work in order to live. Still others may drift between their family home and a life on the street throughout their childhood.

The reason for children starting to live on the street may not solely be poverty and the need to find a way to earn a living; they may also leave home because of violence and abuse perpetrated by their parents. In her study of Indonesian street children, Beazley (2000) argues that this rejection of the 'family' is part of the perceived 'problem' of street children: 'their very presence is a challenge to the state's development philosophy and the ideological construction of the ideal family, home and child, which it uses for social control' (2000: 195). Having left home, however, these **working children** often develop their own **youth** subcultures that are characterised by a particular 'system of values, beliefs, hierarchies and language' – in short, a subculture that provides them with a positive self-identity and sense of belonging (2000: 196).

Given the stigma attached to being a street child in Indonesia, and the shame that the children experience if they do return home, Beazley argues that the street provides a **space** 'where an alienated child is able to survive, and to feel as though he [*sic*] exists in a world that would rather he did not' (2000: 208). However, as Gigengack (2008) reminds us, there is a danger in over-romanticising the lives that children lead on the street. This other social world is neither necessarily safe nor free from abuse; his research in Mexico City revealed that many street children adopt self-destructive lifestyles, such as taking drugs or inhaling solvents, which result in their early death.

The phenomenon of street children should not be seen as solely a problem of the majority South. Street children also exist in more affluent societies; for example, in the UK, children also work on the street as rent-boys or prostitutes. However, significantly, those who live on the streets in these more affluent societies are more usually referred to as 'runaways' or 'homeless'. This rephrasing works in some ways to create the illusion that the 'problem' of street children is a problem that only the developing countries in the majority South have to face. However, research sponsored by the Consortium for Street Children (2003) about street children in the UK shows that their reasons for leaving home mirror those of street children elsewhere, and that the risks they face to their health and **welfare** are also comparable.

Not only do street children raise problems for governments, they also alert us to many of the issues that **childhood studies** addresses about the **social construction** of childhood, children's **competence** and **needs** by reminding us of the enormous **diversity** of children's lives and experiences across the world.

FURTHER READING

Beazley, H. (2000) 'Home sweet home? Street-children's sites of belonging', in S.L. Holloway and G. Valentine (eds), *Children's Geographies*. London: Routledge.

Consortium for Street Children (2003) *Briefing Paper: Street Children in the United Kingdom*. London: Consortium for Street Children.

Gigengack, R. (2008) 'Critical omissions: Reading the street children studies from a street-ethnographic perspective', in P. Christensen and A. James (eds), *Research with Children* (2nd edn). London: Falmer.

Glauser, B. (1997) 'Street children: Deconstructing a construct', in A. James and A. Prout (eds), *Constructing and Reconstructing Childhood* (2nd edn). London: Falmer.

Structure

Social structure refers to the social institutions and relational components of the social fabric around which societies are organised. These delineate the processes through which social relations are organised and transacted, and from which each society derives its identity.

structure

127

Understanding and analysing the composition and nature of social structure has been a central element in the development of sociology as a social science discipline, and one that has generated sustained debate and disagreement. The details of this debate are too complex to engage with here but its existence must be acknowledged, as must the fact that there are few agreed definitions of what precisely social structure is and how it is constituted. The definition offered above may well be challenged, therefore, by other sociologists.

What this definition seeks to do, however, is to highlight two important elements of social structure as a concept used within **childhood studies**. The first is that each and every society is built around various social institutions, the precise nature of which will vary among societies but which will be physically and organisationally present in all societies. Such institutions include the law (however it may be organised), represented as a system of rules and related mechanisms for social control (e.g. courts, police etc.); economic and political institutions such as banks and stock markets, systems of government, and rules for governance and **citizenship**; and religious institutions, including not only places of worship but a system of organising religious beliefs and some form of identifiable religious leaders or leadership.

The second, less tangible but no less important, element is relational; in other words, every society also has particular ways of structuring and conducting social relations. These will include moral and ethical systems (which are often but not necessarily derived from religious institutions), and various ways of grouping people according to certain shared characteristics; in other words, social organisation. Such groupings might include, for example, class, **gender**, **ethnicity**, **generation** or other systems of social stratification, including **childhood** itself, through which social relations and transactions take place.

Within the debate about social structure, the **family** (however defined and understood) deserves particular mention. It is not only part of both the institutional and relational elements of social structure, playing a crucial role in mediating between the two, but it also mediates between the individual and the wider society to which each individual belongs. It is also important because both institutional and relational elements are essential to the process of **socialisation** and therefore to social and cultural reproduction: that is, the means by which societies ensure their continuity.

The importance of understanding social structure in the study of **childhood** is that sociology, as a discipline, examines the influence of social structure in determining who we are and how we behave. In other words, childhood exists in a social **space** that is defined by law, politics, religion, economics and so on, and within this social space, the nature of childhood is further influenced by social class, generation, gender, ethnicity, and so on. Thus, any individual **child** will be the 'product' of powerful external social and institutional forces, shaped by and through the socialisation process and reinforced by daily social transactions that themselves are determined by these same structural elements. That this is so is largely self-evident, but any understanding of childhood, both as a social status and as a lived experience, must incorporate such analytical perspectives. The importance of these structural components of childhood was clearly acknowledged by James et al. (1998) in their discussion of the socially constructed child and the social-structural child.

The major limitation of such perspectives, however, is that they are deterministic; in other words, they suggest that the individual and their identity are little more than the end-product of the combined effect of such social structural forces, transmitted through the process of socialisation. Such sociological determinism can usefully be compared with the psychological determinism represented by **developmental psychology**. One major contribution of **childhood studies** has been to demonstrate that, although it is important to acknowledge the powerful influences that structure exerts on children and their childhoods, within this, children constantly exercise **agency**: they make self-conscious decisions and choices as independent **social actors** that are not determined solely by structure.

Thus the relationship between structure and agency has long been debated within sociology and remains central today (Martin and Dennis, 2010). Understanding this relationship is, however, also core to our understanding of the production and reproduction of childhood, of the lived experiences of different childhoods, and of the **cultural politics** of childhood. While the study of structure emphasises the commonalities of childhood and the elements of social life that children share, the focus on agency emphasises the **diversity** of individual childhoods and the importance of recognising children as social actors, with all that this implies about their **competence**, **citizenship**, **participation** and **rights**.

FURTHER READING

Frønes, I. (2005) 'Structuration of childhood: An essay on the structuring of childhood and anticipatory socialisation', in J. Qvortrup (ed.), *Studies in Modern Childhood: Society, Agency and Culture*. Basingstoke: Palgrave Macmillan.

James, A. and James, A.L. (2004) *Constructing Childhood: Theory, Policy and Social Practice*. London: Palgrave Macmillan.

James, A., Jenks, C. and Prout, A. (1998) *Theorising Childhood*. Cambridge: Polity.

Martin, P.J. and Dennis, A. (2010) *Human Agents and Social Structures*. Manchester: Manchester University Press.

Qvortrup, J. and Kjørholt, A-T. (eds) (2011) *The Modern Child and the Flexible Labour Market: Early Childhood Education and Care*. Basingstoke: Palgrave Macmillan.

United Nations Convention on the Rights of the Child (UNCRC)

*An international convention, adopted almost around the world, that defines the rights of any child, anywhere, regardless of race, creed or culture (see also entry for **Rights**).*

The above definition of the UNCRC gives an idea of the enormity of the task faced by those who drafted it, a task faced previously by their predecessors who drafted the Declaration of the Rights of the Child, which was adopted by the League of Nations (the forerunner of the United Nations) at Geneva in 1924, and subsequently the Declaration of the Rights of the Child, adopted in 1959 by the General Assembly of the United Nations. The Declaration of Geneva was a much more straightforward document than the UNCRC. It contained only five principles that addressed very basic issues, such as the right of hungry children to be fed and of sick children to be nursed. The 1959 Declaration went further by outlining ten principles but, as a declaration, the rights listed did not represent legal obligations on States Parties.

The origins of the UNCRC lie in a request from UNICEF to the UN General Assembly, to which it responded in 1976 when it declared that 1979 would be the International Year of the Child. In the run up to this landmark event, the government of Poland submitted a draft proposal for a new convention on the rights of the **child** to the UN Commission on Human Rights in 1978 in the somewhat unrealistic hope, when viewed with the wisdom of hindsight, that it would be adopted as an internationally binding document in 1979. Anxious to avoid the shortcomings of previous attempts to address the issue of children's rights, it took the UN a further ten years of discussion until the final draft of the new Convention was completed, before being approved in 1989 by the Committee on Human Rights. It was finally approved by the General Assembly on 20 November 1989, and came into effect in September 1990.

In the event, the UNCRC has become the most widely ratified of any UN convention: at the time of writing, every country in the world has signed the Convention and all but two, the USA and Somalia, have ratified it. In terms of global politics, this gives the UNCRC a highly significant profile on the world stage. Arguably, however, its main importance lies in the sheer breadth of its vision, defining, as it does, a set of rights that, having taken account of the diverse traditions and cultural values of States Parties in relation to the **protection** and development of the child, are nonetheless intended to be applied to *all* children, wherever they may be born and wherever they may live.

The UNCRC is intended to be a legally binding instrument, international in its application, which, in its in 54 Articles and 2 Optional Protocols, sets out to incorporate the full range of human rights for children, including their civil, cultural, economic, political and social rights. These rights are organised around four core principles: non-discrimination; devotion to the **best interests** of the child; the right to life, survival and development; and respect for the views of the child. Part I contains 40 Articles outlining these rights, while Part II contains a further 4 Articles outlining the *way* the Convention is intended to operate through the establishment of a Committee of experts, the role of which is to monitor the implementation of the Convention.

There is a broad consensus that the rights encompassed by the UNCRC can be grouped under three main headings:

- *Provision rights*, which are intended to enable children's growth and development, such as their rights to food, housing, education.
- *Prevention/protection rights*, which require States Parties to put systems in place to prevent the abuse of children or infringements of the rights they do have (e.g. to privacy, or to family life) and to protect them against exploitation/abuse.
- **Participation** *rights*, enabling children to take part in decisions made on their behalf, to hold an opinion, and to have freedom of conscience.

It is interesting to note that the two Protocols that are optional for States Parties relate to the involvement of children in armed conflict, and the sale of children, child prostitution and child pornography.

In order to embrace such a broad range of concerns and to gather the unprecedented degree of international support that it has, the Convention outlines a set of *necessarily* generally worded rights. In addition, States Parties were allowed to make declarations and enter reservations when adopting the Convention that enabled them to exempt themselves from any provisions they specified; for example, where they had concerns about conflicts between the rights specified in the Convention and their religious laws and teachings. The difficulty of adequately addressing different cultural contexts and traditions in the UNCRC is also reflected in the emergence of regional versions, such as the African Charter on the Rights and Welfare of the Child, and even this had difficulty in achieving acceptance within the Organisation of African Unity. Egypt, for example, rejected provisions relating to adoption and the minimum **age** of marriage as being contrary to Islamic Law.

A further weakness lies in the fact that although the UNCRC is legally binding, in the absence of the establishment of an international tribunal that is competent to deal with breaches of the Convention by States Parties, it is not legally enforceable. A child whose rights under the Convention have been infringed has no recourse to any legal remedy and therefore breaches of children's rights by States Parties go unsanctioned. Compliance is, however, monitored by the UN Committee on the Rights of the Child. This requires States Parties to submit periodic reports on their progress in implementing the Convention, sometimes leading to very critical comments and recommendations. However, the generation of moral pressure on States Parties that have fallen short of their obligations does not amount to effective enforcement.

Of the two countries that have signed but not ratified the UNCRC, Somalia has no effective government. The USA, however, has been highly critical of the idea of children's rights and has refused to accept its obligations under the Convention, arguing that it is not the only, nor the necessarily best, way of ensuring the development of policies and programmes to benefit children. Indeed, in spite of President Obama commenting during his campaign prior to being elected in 2008 that he thought it embarrassing for the USA to be alone in the world with Somalia in not ratifying the UNCRC, the very idea of children as holders of rights is still widely viewed as a threat to the right of American parents to direct the upbringing and education of their children.

The UNCRC has undoubtedly led to many improvements in the lives of children around the world but, because of the very real practical difficulties in its effective enforcement and the need to embrace such a diverse range of political and cultural contexts, critics have argued that it has not had the impact that was desired or intended by the UN. Moreover, because of its origins in the western industrialised world, it embodies a particularly European perspective on **childhood**. It has, however, undoubtedly triggered a wide-ranging international debate about children and their childhoods and has assumed a powerful symbolic role in the context of such debates, with some suggesting that, in spite of these criticisms, the UNCRC and the associated debate has seen the emergence of the global child.

FURTHER READING

Fortin, J. (2003) *Children's Rights and the Developing Law* (2nd edn). London: LexisNexis/ Butterworths.

Franklin, B. (ed.) (2002) *The New Handbook of Children's Rights: Comparative Policy and Practice.* London: Routledge.

Grugel, J. and Piper, N. (2007) *Critical Perspectives on Global Governance: Rights and Regulations in Governing Regimes.* London: Routledge.

Hodgkin, R. and Newell, P. (2007) *Implementation Handbook for the Convention on the Rights of the Child* (3rd edn). Geneva: UNICEF.

James, A. and James, A.L. (2004) *Constructing Childhood: Theory, Policy and Social Practice.* London: Palgrave Macmillan. (See especially Ch. 4)

Liebel, M. (2012) *Children's Rights from Below: Cross-Cultural Perspectives.* Basingstoke: Palgrave Macmillan.

Percy-Smith, B. and Thomas, N. (eds) (2010) *A Handbook of Children and Young People's Participation: Perspectives from Theory and Practice.* London: Routledge.

Twum-Danso, A. (2009) 'Reciprocity, respect and responsibility: The 3rs underlying parent–child relationships in Ghana and the implications for children's rights', *The International Journal of Children's Rights*, 17(3): 415–32.

Van Bueren, G. (2007) *Child Rights in Europe.* Strasbourg Cedex: Council of Europe. (To access the full text of the convention, go to: www2.ohchr.org/english/law/crc.htm)

Vulnerability

> *A state of weakness, of being at risk from harm and therefore in need of protection.*

Vulnerability is a concept that has little or no specific meaning in the absence of some qualifying condition: in other words, a person or a thing is only vulnerable in relation to something specific. Thus a castle may be strong in terms of its fortifications but vulnerable in terms of a siege; an army may be strong in terms of its size but vulnerable to guerrilla attacks; or a person may currently be strong physically or mentally but vulnerable to, for example, imminent attack from behind or a long-term predisposition to senile dementia. Vulnerability is therefore a concept that generally only derives its meaning when considered in the context of specific risks that raise the prospect of immediate or longer-term harm, and which may therefore require some kind of protective action if any is available.

There is an important sense, however, in which all children are seen as vulnerable and in which childhood is seen as a period of inherent vulnerability because of the perceived **innocence** and lack of **competence** of children, as a result of which they are thought to require **protection**. Such thinking is implicit in biological and psychological **developmentalism**, which implies that, because the child is not yet fully developed, it is vulnerable to any adverse influences that may disrupt the 'normal' completion of the developmental process.

It is clear that to some considerable extent such a view is valid, in that a very young child is physically immature and may be less well able to protect itself against physical harms such as assault by an older child or an adult. Similarly, a young child may be tempted to act in a way that is inappropriate or dangerous because it lacks the experience or psychological **maturity** to assess adequately the risk or resist the temptation. What is more problematic, however, is the idea that all children are vulnerable, that all of their childhoods and the entire period of childhood are risky, and that all children, therefore, need the same level of protection from the same risks.

As with **poverty** and **welfare**, the issue of vulnerability in relation to children and **childhood** is substantially determined by historical, cultural, geographical, political and economic variables. What constitutes both risk and protection is simultaneously **socially constructed** and helps to formulate our understandings of childhood. Thus, for example, if, in a particular historical and cultural context, children's **health** and future development are seen to be put at risk by being required to undertake 'dangerous' and 'demanding' **work**, they will be seen to be vulnerable. It is also likely that they will be seen as in need of protection by adults, by society or by the law. In a different context, however, children engaging in precisely the same form of work may be regarded as making an important economic contribution to their family, learning important life and social skills and developing the competences they require to become full adult members of society. Thus, as our understandings of childhood and what it means to be a child change in response to political, social or economic developments, so it is likely that the parameters adults use to define risk, vulnerability and protection will also change.

Perhaps one of the key foci for the study of childhood should be the analysis of such defining processes and the way in which these affect our understandings and **representations** of children and childhood (Christensen, 2000). Exploring how children experience this cultural construction of themselves as necessarily vulnerable is also critical, for as Christensen points out in her analysis of children's experiences of illness, this 'forms an element of the cultural learning of children' (2000: 57).

Understanding how ideas of vulnerability are expressed and experienced will also give us important clues to the changes that are taking place in society. Such issues are clearly evident in the context of recent developments in the UK, for example. Recent government policies in relation to the delivery of services to children identify five positive outcomes relating to aspects of children's physical, psychological and emotional well-being that are seen as central to their 'successful' development (James and James, 2008), or rather their development into successful adults. In this particular context, a 'successful' adult is defined by implication as one who engages fully in the labour market, is politically active and is socially responsible. Thus, a raft of social policies and State interventions have been promulgated in order to 'protect' children from the 'risk' of not achieving these outcomes, outcomes that reflect a very particular understanding of vulnerability and thus of the nature of children and childhood.

Increasingly, as concerns about the risks to and vulnerability of children become universalised in the debate about children's **rights**, we are likely to see other examples of the reappraisal of the vulnerability of children and of the meanings of childhood.

FURTHER READING

Bradshaw, J. and Mayhew, E. (eds) (2005) *The Well-being of Children in the UK* (2nd edn). London: Save the Children.

Christensen, P. (2000) 'Childhood and the cultural constitution of vulnerable bodies', in A. Prout (ed.), *The Body, Childhood and Society*. Basingstoke: Macmillan.

Franklin, B. (ed.) (2002) *The Handbook of Children's Rights: Comparative Policy and Practice*. London: Routledge.

James, A.L. and James, A. (2008) 'Changing childhood in the UK: Reconstructing discourses of "risk" and "protection"', in A. James and A.L. James (eds), *European Childhoods: Cultures, Politics and Childhoods in Europe*. London: Palgrave Macmillan.

Jensen, A-M., Ben-Arieh, A., Conti, C., Kutsar, D., Phádraig, M.N.G. and Nielsen, H.W. (eds) (2004) *Children's Welfare in Ageing Europe*, Vols I and II. Trondheim: NOSEB.

UNICEF (2007) *Child Poverty in Perspective: An Overview of Child Well-being in Rich Countries*. Innocenti Report Card 7, UNICEF Innocenti Research Centre. Florence: United Nations Children's Fund.

Welfare

The state of well-being or services provided to ensure the well-being of others.

'Welfare' is a term that has a general, common-sense meaning which is implicit in the word itself: it is about faring well. In the latter part of the 20th century, however, it is a term that came to assume particular significance in the context of the development of political systems and States that have been founded on, or organised around, the principles of welfare. Such States sought to ensure that their citizens were guaranteed certain minimum standards of living (e.g. in terms of health care, education, and pension support for older citizens) and were protected from the adversities that could be suffered, particularly in capitalist economic systems, in times of hardship and economic downturn (e.g. in terms of unemployment benefits and other forms of social security).

The development of such welfare systems has been taken the furthest in the countries of western Europe and, in particular, in Scandinavia. These have stood in marked contrast to other western countries, such as the USA, where the welfare net has been far less effective in terms of its spread and the nature of provisions, and where private sector involvement in the form of health insurance, for example, has restricted access to good-quality health care for the poorer members of the community. In many countries in the majority South, however, even basic welfare provisions, including those for children, are often rudimentary.

More recently, however, what was once an entirely positive concept has also begun to be associated with critiques that have emerged of welfare provision. Thus, for example, an issue of growing political concern in many welfare-state systems has been the growing crisis in welfare capitalism: in other words, the grow-ing burden of the cost of welfare provision on various countries' gross domestic product (GDP). With changing demographics and, in many European countries, a growing proportion of elderly people being supported by a shrinking working population, coupled with declining birth rates (Jensen et al., 2004), this cost is becoming increasingly difficult to meet through traditional welfare systems. The result is that in many countries there has been increasing development of so-called 'mixed economies of welfare' based on increased private-sector involvement in the provision of various welfare services.

A further critique that has emerged, particularly but by no means exclusively from neo-conservative economics, and one that is not entirely unrelated to alarm about the rising costs of welfare provision, relates to the potential adverse effects of welfare provision in terms of its ability to create dependency amongst recipients of welfare. In other words, there is concern that generous levels of welfare provi-sion reduce the incentive to seek paid employment. Questions of welfare at the macro level of State provision and politics revolve around issues of both ideology and of relative **poverty** and welfare. They also involve complex political and eco-nomic judgements about norms and minimum standards in terms of quality of life that are deemed to be acceptable, or can be tolerated, in any given society.

At the micro level, however, assessments by individuals of what factors comprise an acceptable standard of living and acceptable levels of welfare are likely to vary considerably, not only within societies but particularly between different societies. Once basic **needs** have been met, the ways in which individuals define, determine and construct their own welfare and well-being are likely to vary considerably, depending upon a wide range of personal and cultural factors, and the social, eco-nomic and political contexts in which they live. Thus welfare, like poverty, is not an absolute but a relative concept.

The significance of welfare in terms of the social study of childhood is that, as with so much else, children are seldom in a position to determine what con-stitutes their own welfare. They are rarely consulted by adults in order to deter-mine their views and understandings of what might be for their welfare or in their **best interests**. This is, in part, a reflection of the dominant view of adults that children lack the **competence** to understand and decide about such issues, that they lack the experience to know how their **needs** can best be met, and that because they are developmentally incomplete they are therefore **vulnerable**. Indeed, part of the **protection** adults give to children assumes that they, rather than children, should determine what is in children's best interests, how their welfare needs should be met, and how best to make provision for these, as

Parton (2006) shows in his detailing of the ways in which this has occurred in England over the last 30 years.

Any **rights** that children have in relation to their own welfare thus become the **responsibility** of adults to meet. Such an approach is clearly evident in the provisions and wording of the United Nations Convention on the Rights of the Child (**UNCRC**) 1989. The Convention frames children's rights and welfare in terms of protection, arguing in the Preamble that 'the child, by reason of his [*sic*] physical and mental immaturity, needs special safeguards and care, including legal protection, before as well as after birth'. Apart from the responsibilities given directly to them by the Convention for ensuring the welfare of children, all States who have signed up to the Convention are also required by Article 5 to respect

> the responsibilities, rights and duties of parents or, where applicable, members of the extended family or community as provided for by local custom … to provide, in a manner consistent with the evolving capacities of the child, appropriate direction and guidance in the exercise by the child of the rights recognized in the present Convention.

The Convention is therefore an important instrument in terms of the global drive to ensure that minimum standards are met in terms of provisions for children's welfare. It is equally important for the stress placed in Article 3 on the need to make the child's best interests the primary (although not the only and not the first or paramount) consideration in all actions concerning children. Although Article 12 also makes important provisions for the participation of children in decisions that affect them, the thrust of the Convention is that defining and providing for the welfare of children are the responsibility of adults.

Welfare is thus an important concept in the social study of childhood, not only because of its intrinsic importance in determining the lived experiences of children, but also because it gives us important insights into the structuring of relationships between adults and children.

FURTHER READING

Bradshaw, J. and Mayhew, E. (eds) (2005) *The Well-being of Children in the UK* (2nd edn). London: Save the Children.

Esping-Andersen, G. (1990) *The Three Worlds of Welfare Capitalism*. Cambridge: Polity.

Esping-Andersen, G., Gallie, D., Hemerijck, A. and Myles, J. (2002) *Why We Need a New Welfare State*. Oxford: Oxford University Press.

Franklin, B. (ed.) (2002) *The Handbook of Children's Rights: Comparative Policy and Practice*. London: Routledge.

Jensen, A-M., Ben-Arieh, A., Conti, C., Kutsar, D., Phádraig, M.N.G. and Nielsen, H.W. (eds) (2004) *Children's Welfare in Ageing Europe*, Vols I and II. Trondheim: NOSEB.

Parton, N. (2006) *Safeguarding Children: Early Intervention and Surveillance in a Late Modern Society*. Basingstoke: Palgrave Macmillan.

UNICEF (2007) *Child Poverty in Perspective: An Overview of Child Well-being in Rich Countries*. Innocenti Report Card 7, UNICEF Innocenti Research Centre. Florence: United Nations Children's Fund.

Work and Working Children

Children who contribute their labour, either on an unpaid basis or for monetary gain; they may or may not combine this activity with education.

The concept 'working children' is one that in recent years has become the preferred way of describing children who carry out the kinds of activities that used to be glossed by the terms 'child labour' or 'child work' (Boyden et al., 1998). The reason for this shift in definition is the difficulty in sustaining the distinction between 'work' and 'labour' in the face of changing ideas not only about the nature and **representation** of **childhood**, but also as a result of research that has sought out the views of children who work.

Up until the 1980s, the term 'child labour' was traditionally used to describe all the kinds of adult work activities that children carried out. Mistakenly thought only to be associated with children living in the majority South (there are examples of children doing such work in Northern industrialised countries too), child labour was condemned as being incompatible with childhood. It was seen as exploitative and as damaging to children's social, physical and psychological development. Work that fell within this category included bonded labour, where parents might 'bond' their children's capacity as workers to an employer to pay off a debt for a shorter or longer period of time; slavery, which might involve parents selling their children to a slave master for profit; and small-scale, unregulated sweat-shop work, where children would be employed for long hours in bad working conditions. Often this work involved small-scale factory work, carried out in dangerous workshops where there were few regulations about the hours or working conditions that children endured.

However, sometimes the term 'child labour' was used more broadly to include other kinds of work done by children, including work on family farms, care of siblings or general household work. This kind of work was not considered as exploitative and, indeed, was even regarded as having a broadly educative function. Thus, while there was universal condemnation over the worst forms of child labour (work that violates children's **health** and **welfare**), beyond that the other work children engage in began to be judged rather differently, depending on the social context and the type of work.

Boyden et al. (1998) employ the term 'working children' as a more encompassing term that can avoid the moral judgement that is implicitly drawn on in the distinction between (good) work and (bad) labour. Referring to children working in the majority South, they identify four categories of working children:

1   children in rural areas who perform unpaid work for their families;

2   children who do domestic work, either unpaid in their own homes or for employees;

3 children who work in the informal sector in small shops or back street workshops, or street children who make their living through, for example, windscreen washing, begging or prostitution;

4 children who work in the formal economy in industrial or commercial outlets. (Boyden et al., 1998: 23–6)

Out of this wide range of working children, it is the children working in the informal sector who are popularly held by western media to represent working children. Yet these children constitute the minority of working children worldwide and they may not, in fact, be the worst off. The largest numbers of working children are instead to be found in the domestic and agricultural sectors, and many of these children may also suffer great hardship and abuse, even though they are working within familial-based contexts.

The term 'working children' is also useful because, as is now widely recognised, many children who work also go to **school**. Indeed, they may have to work in order to go to school since in many countries in the majority South schooling is not free. Thus, as Boyden et al. (1998) note, the frequent call from rich industrialised countries for the abolition of child work in order to free children to go to school may not be helpful. The loss of opportunities for work may, for some children, mean the loss of educational opportunities also. In addition, given that children's contribution to a family's income may be substantial (estimates are as high as 50 per cent in some cases), preventing children from undertaking paid work may increase family **poverty**. This would leave children more impoverished and at greater risk of destitution and malnourishment than if they had continued to work. In many contexts, the best solution is for there to be some flexibility in the school system so that children are able to combine work with education – as has happened, for example, for children working in the Nepalese carpet industry. For many children also, learning a trade early in life may offer them better prospects for their future adult life, since schooling that might be locally available to them may only be of poor quality.

Given the wide variety of work that children undertake and the difficulties of definition, calculating the population of working children is extremely difficult and estimates vary wildly. However, it is important to remember that many children who live in more affluent countries also work, albeit that in these contexts regulations exist to restrict the kinds and hours of work a child can do according to **age**. Children's work is therefore not always the function of necessity; it is often a matter of choice. In the UK, for example, it is better-off middle-class children, rather than poorer working-class children, who have the most experience of work, usually taking jobs in the retail and service sectors of the economy. Mizen et al. (2001) show, for example, that children enjoy working and value the opportunities for socialising and exercising the **responsibility** and independence that work can bring, in addition to the economic benefits that accrue. Interestingly, although it has been argued that working may be detrimental to children's schoolwork, research by McKechnie and Hobbs (2001) has shown that those children who do up to five hours of work a week often have a better attendance record at school and better attainment than their non-working counterparts. Poorer children who worked longer hours did, however, perform less well at school.

Children in affluent countries also do domestic work within the **family**, such as cleaning, baby-sitting, running errands and other small household jobs which, Morrow (1994) argues, also have to be considered as work. When children undertake these tasks, they are also contributing to the wider economy, since they are carrying out work that would otherwise have to be done by adults. In addition, changes in adult work patterns, with more mothers going out to work, mean that more children are taking on these tasks. In a similar vein, Qvortrup (1995) has argued that school-work should also be seen as a form of child work. Compelled by law to attend school as part of a diachronic division of labour, children's participation in schooling represents a form of embodied social capital, an investment in the future of society.

Another invisible form of work that some children do is caring work. This work has often been invisible and not considered as work, even though sibling care (whereby older children look after younger brothers and sisters) is, in the majority South, often a key feature of children's everyday life. In addition, until very recently the role that child carers play in looking after sick or disabled parents has gone unrecognised. This work can be physically and emotionally difficult and demanding, involving intimate personal care in addition to general household tasks. In the UK, for example, up until 1995 children were denied access to state benefits designed to help those in caring roles since, as children and not adults, they were not deemed eligible to make a claim. Following the Carers Act 1995, this situation improved somewhat, since the Act gave local authorities a duty to address the needs of young carers. However, as Becker et al. (2001) point out, despite this new legislation, the help that child carers get from the State may in some cases still be insufficient.

Research on working children underscores, therefore, the **diversity** of children's lives and also highlights a range of issues about the **social construction** of childhood in relation to concepts of children's development, welfare and **competence**. Like **street children** and **child soldiers**, working children are participating in adult **spaces**, often with few allowances made for their being children.

FURTHER READING

Becker, S., Dearden, C. and Aldridge, J. (2001) 'Children's labour of love? Young carers and care work', in P. Mizen, C. Pole and A. Burton (eds), *Hidden Hands: International Perspectives on Children's Work and Labour*. London: Routledge/Falmer.

Bourdillon, M.F.C. (2005) 'Working children in Zimbabwe', in L.E. Bass (ed.), *Sociological Studies of Childhood and Youth*, Vol. 10. London: Elsevier.

Boyden, J., Ling, B. and Myers, W. (1998) *What Works for Working Children*. Stockholm: Rädda Barnen/UNICEF.

McKecknie, J. and Hobbs, S. (2001) 'Work and education: Are they compatible for children and adolescents?', in P. Mizen, C. Pole and A. Burton (eds), *Hidden Hands: International Perspectives on Children's Work and Labour*. London: Routledge/Falmer.

Mizen, P., Pole, C. and Bolton, A. (2001) 'Why be a school-age worker?', in P. Mizen, C. Pole and A. Burton (eds), *Hidden Hands: International Perspectives on Children's Work and Labour*. London: Routledge/Falmer.

work and working children

Morrow, V. (1994) 'Responsible children? Aspects of children's work and employment outside school in contemporary UK', in B. Mayall (ed.), *Children's Childhoods Observed and Experienced*. London: Falmer.

Qvortrup, J. (1995) 'From useful to useful: The historical continuity of children's constructive participation', in A. Ambert (ed.), *Sociological Studies of Children*, Vol. 7. Greenwich, CT: JAI Press.

Youth

A young person who is too old to be regarded socially as just a child – usually but not necessarily a teenager – but who is not yet legally an adult; also a period in the life-course that is situated between childhood and adulthood.

The word 'youth' is interesting because as our definition suggests, unlike **child**, it is used to describe both an individual at a particular stage in their life-course and a social category, the equivalent to which for child is **childhood**. In its **social construction** in western industrialised countries, it is linked not only to chronological **age**, loosely defining that period between the ages of 13 and 18, but also to physical development (describing the period of rapid growth associated with the onset of puberty and adolescence) and social development. Youth therefore describes the period of transition between childhood and adulthood that is often associated with social experimentation, the emergence from the **family**, and the development of the social self and of social identity. It is, in many senses, the period of social apprenticeship during which the individual is expected to prepare for and gradually learn the economic and social skills and capacities associated with adulthood.

Because of the transitions associated with youth, it is often associated with rebellion. Moving away from the family (both psychologically and socially), youth may move towards the **peer group** as the increasingly dominant reference point for behaviours, values and attitudes. Linked to throwing over the relative conformity of childhood, this life-stage may involve testing the established conventions of adulthood. It is no accident, therefore, that **delinquency** is most commonly a term associated with youth. These facets of youth as a social construct highlight something very important: the conceptual ambiguity of youth and the ambivalence of adults towards youth.

These are compounded by the fact that although historically the transition from childhood to adulthood, and thus the period described as youth, was relatively short, with clearly defined and culturally prescribed rites of passage to mark the transition, this is no longer the case in late modernity. In most western industrialised countries, with the increasing emphasis on education, the period of social and economic dependency of children on adults has become increasingly prolonged.

This has effectively expanded both the social and temporal **space** of youth. At the same time, however, the **age** at which the physical growth association with puberty commences has become progressively lower. Thus youth as a social space and a stage in the life-course has grown.

In order to address this problem, increasingly commentators and politicians have resorted to distinguishing between children and young people. At the same time, however, we are left with a broad consensus that the age of majority, at which full adulthood and citizenship commence, is about 18 and that for the purposes of children's **rights**, a child is any person below that age. Thus in the global debate about children's rights, youth as both a social and a legal category does not exist. Yet in terms of the debate about children's rights to participation, most efforts are directed at older children – youths or young people. This is partly because of their greater developmental **maturity** and partly out of recognition of the fact that youth is a period of social apprenticeship and that the learning which comes from participation is good preparation for eventual **citizenship**.

For **childhood studies**, this has created a dilemma that is often not directly acknowledged and is little studied. In marking out childhood as an important and neglected area of study, which has highlighted the need to recognise children as **social actors**, it has been necessary to emphasise the distinction between childhood and adulthood, to explore the boundaries between them and, at the same time, to avoid the fragmentation that might result from a more nuanced analysis of the social space of childhood.

It is widely acknowledged, however, that it makes little sense to conceive of adulthood as a single undifferentiated social category and a single stage in the life-course when demographic, psychological, economic and social analyses all tell us that the different phases of adult life (young adults, newly married couples, new parents, middle age, late-middle age, retirement, old age, dependent old age) are each so different, and are each experienced so differently, that they need to be studied in their own right as well as part of the 'whole' of adulthood. Similarly, therefore, it makes little sense to conceive of childhood in the same way and to ignore the important differences between infancy, early years, early school years, the 'tweens' and youth. The difficulty for childhood studies is that, if too great an emphasis is placed on such distinctions, we will fall into the trap of reinforcing those perspectives derived from **developmental psychology** that serve to undermine or deny children's **agency** and rights and therefore the unique contribution of childhood studies.

At the same time, it is also necessary to recognise that youth is already considered for some important purposes to be separate and distinct from childhood. Thus, for example, many countries have separate youth justice systems that are designed to be responsive to the special considerations which arise when dealing with those who are not children and therefore not criminally responsible, and yet not yet adult and therefore not fully responsible. Many countries have separate youth policies for dealing with the particular educational, economic, health and social care issues associated with youth, and in many countries youth studies has emerged academically as a discrete and largely separate area of research and higher education, partly but not exclusively because of the prevailing social construction of youth as a distinct and unique stage in the life-course.

FURTHER READING

Alanen, L. and Mayall, B. (eds) (2001) *Conceptualizing Child–Adult Relations*. London: Routledge/Falmer.

Bennett, A., Cieslik, M. and Miles, S. (eds) (2003) *Researching Youth*. London: Palgrave.

Cohen, P. (1997) *Rethinking the Youth Question*. London: Macmillan.

France, A. (2007) *Understanding Youth in Late Modernity*. Maidenhead: Open University Press/McGraw-Hill Education.

Hunt, S. (2005) *The Life Course: A Sociological Introduction*. Basingstoke: Palgrave Macmillan.

MacDonald, R. (ed.) (1997) *Youth, the 'Underclass' and Social Exclusion*. London: Routledge.